The Catawba County Library
Newton. N. C

S0-CGP-207

AMERICAN SAINTS & SEERS

Also by Edward Rice

THE PROPHETIC GENERATION

THE MAN IN THE SYCAMORE TREE

MOTHER INDIA'S CHILDREN

TEMPLE OF THE PHALLIC KING

THE FIVE GREAT RELIGIONS

JOHN FRUM HE COME

THE GANGES

JOURNEY TO UPOLU

MARX, ENGELS, AND THE WORKERS OF THE WORLD

TEN RELIGIONS OF THE EAST

EASTERN DEFINITIONS

BABYLON, NEXT TO NINEVEH

EDWARD RICE

AMERICAN SAINTS & SEERS

AMERICAN-BORN RELIGIONS & THE GENIUS BEHIND THEM

FOUR WINDS PRESS ☆ NEW YORK

'ACKNOWLEDGMENTS

The author is especially indebted to Concetta Clarke, Susan Griffin, and Susan Daniels of the Hampton Library, Bridgehampton, New York, for assistance in obtaining reference material, and also to Rhonda Buttacavoli of the Suffolk Cooperative Library System, who was unusually persistent in tracking down obscure works. Bill Powers of *Corrections Magazine* was generous in supplying information and photographs about the Muslims.

LIBRARY OF CONGRESS CATALOGING IN PUBLICATION DATA

Rice, Edward.
   American saints and seers.

   Bibliography: p.
   Includes index.
   Summary: Discusses a variety of religions that were nurtured and grew up on this continent showing a distinct American character with little European influence. Included are the Shakers, Mormons, Christian Scientists, Muslims, and others.
   1. Christian sects—United States—Juvenile literature. 2. United States—Religion—Juvenile literature. 3. Cults—United States—Juvenile literature. [1. Sects—United States. 2. Cults—United States. 3. United States—Religion] I. Title.
BR516.5.R53   291.'.973   81-15293
ISBN 0-590-07581-0   AACR2

PUBLISHED BY FOUR WINDS PRESS

A DIVISION OF SCHOLASTIC INC., NEW YORK, N.Y.

COPYRIGHT © 1982 BY EDWARD RICE

ALL RIGHTS RESERVED

PRINTED IN THE UNITED STATES OF AMERICA

LIBRARY OF CONGRESS CATALOG CARD NUMBER: 81-15293

1 2 3 4 5 86 85 84 83 82

112986

CONTENTS

PREFACE

MERICA IS A GOD-OBSESSED NATION. STATISTICS MIGHT show that tens of millions of people claim no religious faith at all, that they aren't interested in one, or that they have left the churches of their parents and their youth. Millions of others, however, are absorbed in the search for the divine, for salvation and redemption, for eternal life and the forgiveness of sins, for God's pardon and God's love. Millions expect His Second Coming in the immediate future. A Gallup poll taken a few years ago showed that 98 percent of all Americans believed in God, though only 40 percent regularly attended a church. Other studies show that America is the most religious nation on earth.

Americans have historically sought the perfect society, most often one based upon religious values. Perfectionism is an

American virtue and an American vice. First the undaunted Pilgrims and Puritans waded through the icy shallows of New England's coast to found perfect, heavenly Jerusalems in the rocky soil. The Quakers, Shakers, Icarians, Mennonites, Rappites, Zoarites, Russellites, Adventists—and countless others—all sought or still do seek the ideal society. The rest of the world is crumbling, they believe, and the godly must prepare for the end. Man is fallible, Americans claim, but he can be perfected with His help.

There is a wonderful, incurable optimism about the sects and churches founded in America. This time the right path, the right way, has been discovered. The sacred texts of the Holy Bible have at last been properly interpreted and understood. The founder, saint, or seer has been given a divine vision that will lead people to a heaven on earth. What is also astonishing is the manner in which the latest American techniques help the faithful along the road. In the nineteenth century, the press in all its forms—magazines, pamphlets, broadsheets, books, and booklets—was a major tool in keeping America religious. Then came radio and the phonograph, and after them television, to bring the message. Finally, there were technological means of keeping track of church members via computers and electronic retrieval systems.

What follows is a brief look at some of the more important, more interesting, and in a few cases even the more scurrilous, of the faiths that were nurtured and grew up on this continent—the "American" churches and sects and cults. All but one of the major churches—the Shakers—are still with us. The Shakers survived almost two centuries before the last aged celibate nonagenarians passed away at Sabbath Lake in Maine. The churches founded abroad and transplanted here—Roman Catholic, Eastern Orthodox, and many Protestant denominations (among them Lutheran, Presbyterian, Baptist, Methodist, Quaker, and those descended from the Anabaptist)—are not part of this book, though all have taken on a coloring and attitudes that reflect the optimism, energy, and technology of their new environment. For an author concerned with the outpouring of the spirit, and *the* Spirit, on native American soil, it is at times distressing to have to set them aside, for they too show manifestations and variations of absorbing interest. How can one easily pass over the fascinating assortment of Baptists—the Landmark Baptists, the Particular Baptists, the Free Will Baptists, the Duck River (and Kindred) Associations of Baptists, the General Six-Principle Baptists, the Primitive Baptists (otherwise "Hard Shell"), the Seventh Day Baptists, the National Baptists Evangelical Life and Soul Saving Assembly of the U.S.A., and so on?

This book is concerned with those faiths born of American soil, as American as apple pie, baseball, the camp meeting, the Hula-Hoop, and the computer. I have concentrated on five important American churches, an amorphous movement known as Pentecostalism, three American Indian faiths, and a black, Detroit-born version of Islam.

1

☆　☆　☆　☆　☆　☆　☆　☆　☆

INTRODUCTION

MY CAR HAD BROKEN DOWN ON THE HIGHWAY, AND I decided to hitchhike back to town. A shiny, new blue-green van stopped, and the driver motioned to me to get in. Like many of the working people in the farming area in which I live, he had a gigantic dog sitting in the front seat beside him, like some shaggy mute person with pointed ears. This dog was a German shepherd; some people prefer Labradors. I squeezed in beside the dog. The driver, a young man with a blond beard and long hair, started to chat. I made some talk about the weather—it was an unusually cold day. Then he asked me what I did. I told him that I was a writer and a photographer, and had spent a lot of time in the Far East. "Did you ever meet those gurus?" he asked. I said I had, and that in fact I had written a book about gurus and other Hindu holy men.

"I've declared myself for Jesus," said the driver.

"Why for Jesus?" I asked.

"I saw Jesus," he said, after a pause. He gave a rambling explanation. He was now thirty. Three years ago he and a local girl had run away to Key West. The girl was only seventeen. After a few weeks he and the girl began to fight. One day he went into a church to think it over. As he was sitting in a pew absorbed in his thoughts, he saw Jesus in a corner. "I could only see His feet. He was in a cloud, floating above the ground." We discussed his vision. He had indeed seen Jesus, he claimed. So he brought the girl back home and "declared himself for Jesus." I asked him what he did for a living.

"I set up stones for Jesus."

"You mean you're a mason?"

"No. I set up stones for Jesus. Along the highway."

The following summer I was over at the county center, and there was the same man handing out sandwiches from a brown paper bag. He remembered me. "I'm giving out sandwiches for Jesus," he said. I took one. It was peanut butter and grape jelly on a heavy, homemade, whole-wheat bread, wrapped in waxed paper. A lot of people on the street refused his sandwiches, and those that accepted them—he was rather persistent—threw them away when they were down the street.

The Christ-like stonemason is part of an American tradition of prophets and seers who have roamed the American countryside, preaching Jesus, urging the many to seek salvation, warning of the end of the world, and predicting the Second Coming of Jesus. Most are unknown; they hand out leaflets or set up signs (or stones) along the roads. One of the most famous was the American wanderer, John Chapman, otherwise known as Johnnie Appleseed. Chapman was a hero of folklore because he planted apple orchards from seeds. He was a follower of the doctrines of the mystical Swedish prophet Emmanuel Swedenborg. Swedenborg was a scientist and engineer who gave up science at the age of fifty-six and for the next thirty years devoted his time to what he called "visitations" and "illuminations." He claimed to have met, in the spiritual realm, biblical prophets and apostles, as well as such historical figures as Aristotle, Socrates, Caesar, and spirits from other planets. It was John Chapman's self-proclaimed mission to go from town to town, from settler to settler, proclaiming the New Jerusalem coming for man. He planted a lot of trees, made few converts, but it was his calling to tell the world that across the ocean a man touched by God was convinced that "angels must be speaking through me."

Chapman traveled the Midwest a century ago on his lonely mission of prophecy and the call to repentance. Recently I picked up a throwaway in a railroad station. A hand-written message reproduced by offset printing, warned, "Oh! Get right with God before it's too late. You are only one heartbeat from death." It was signed by an E. C. Tiemann of Tulsa, Oklahoma. I could only wonder about the call that reached this far-off man or woman, and how hundreds of copies of the message of repentance had reached the East Coast, scattered through a large metropolitan station like a gentle spring rain. One cannot walk down a city street without being given some kind of message. A flyer from Grace & Truth of Danville, Ohio, put into my hands, asked, "Oh, won't you come to the Savior now? Tomorrow might be too late." And a pamphlet received in the mail, unexpected and unsolicited, warned of the Second Coming. It was from the American Missionary Church of Phoenix, Arizona.

SOON-COMING
WORLD-SHAKING
EVENTS!

TOMORROW'S NEWS TODAY!

ASTOUNDING!

STARTLING!

AS FORETOLD BY—

God Almighty!

And then it told of "Prophecies about today being fulfilled today," and "The coming of Jesus Christ in the clouds of heaven!" and "The rapture of the Church into the air—then into heaven!" Other chapters included "The battle of Armageddon—invasion from space!" and "The millennium—1,000-year reign of Christ on earth!"

These are lonely voices in the wilderness, but they are not alone. From one coast to the other, from north to south, there are prophets calling to the world to awaken, to stop sinning. The call is there for all who listen.

An advertisement in a science fiction magazine: "God's Well. Send a self-addressed envelope." A four-page folder came back shortly. On May 31, 1971, it said, Jesus appeared to a woman named Rev. Stella in Richland, Missouri. Her grammar and capitalization were erratic but the message was clear.

He held his hands over the Well and rays of light came out of his fingers and entered the Well. Then He lifted His arms and blessed the grounds around the well. He said: "Now this well and the grounds are holy. Call this God's Well. Many Miracles will happen here. The blind will see, the deaf will hear, and the crippled will walk again.

Many years ago [she writes] Jesus appeared to her holding a star in His hand. She read the inscription on the star and then had a replica made. The Lucky Star may be purchased at God's Well. The price is five dollars.

Madame Stella's folder included a number of letters from people who had been helped by her powers as a faith healer and psychic. There were cures of arthritis, a slight stroke, "a terrible burning in my chest for six months," "a permanent injury when a truck rolled over me," "several vertebrae deteriorating in my back which gave me much anguish," "back trouble and bad legs . . . ulcers, a ruptured disk and sinus trouble," "severe heart pains and a severe sinus infection," "a hurting all around my neck and in my shoulders, and a shortness of breath," "hardening of the arteries," and so on. But there was more. Not only was L. D. of Jackson, Missouri, cured of constipation, indigestion, and a hernia, but—"I saw Jesus five times." Visitors to the Well have seen others besides Jesus, among them "Moses, Mary, Mother of Christ, Abraham, David, and many other Holy Spirits." The result, the Reverend Stella claimed, is that "Souls are saved; people are healed; prosperity in business and higher salaries; self-confidence restored; peace of mind."

EUROPEAN ROOTS

Few ideas, whether religious or secular, arise without some source, some antecedents, however obscure. Virtually all the themes found in the American churches have their parallels, if not their origins, in European sects of earlier years. These include the rejection of sex among the Shakers, polygamy among the Mormons, and the widespread belief in the end of the world among the millennial denominations.

By the sixteenth century the momentum of the Reformation had reached the lowest social strata, the peasants and workers, who felt that they had the same privilege of interpreting the Gospels according to their own views as did the clergy, nobles, and intellectuals. In this age of excitement, and exploration (Asia, Africa, and the Americas were being discovered), the peasants expected social reforms along with the theological reforms introduced by Luther, Melanchthon, Calvin, Zwingli, and other innovators and interpreters. Various peasant "communist" societies were founded based upon a literal application of the Gospels in social matters. The peasants asked to share property (and often included women as property). They wanted an elected rather than a hereditary feudal government, a separation of church and state, an end to taxes and to interest in loans, and other reforms calculated to help them out of serfdom. They also refused to take oaths in court.

Their theological changes were not startling, but one was to become a major issue—baptism. Individuals, they believed, must be baptized as adults, not as infants, as had been the custom in the Roman Church. This matter had engaged the attention of some of the major Reformers, but it was, in general, the peasants who had made it a central point. Those who were baptized as infants must be rebaptized, the peasant leaders said. The movement came to be known as "Anabaptist," at first a term of scorn and contempt. The Anabaptists raised other questions about the sacrament. The age of the baptized and the form (sprinkling or immersion, one, two, or three immersions) were to assume controversial proportions in many new or "restored" churches in both Europe and America.

The peasant uprisings shook western Europe. The new Protestant leaders, who had so adamantly denied Rome, first tried to understand, then began to put down the peasant communes. In the German states, some hundred thousand rebel Anabaptist peasants were killed and fifty thousand made homeless. The peasant leaders were brutally hanged or burned if captured. Many of the peasants fled to the more tolerant lands of Scandinavia and the Netherlands.

In 1683, a colony of Swiss exiles took refuge in the Netherlands, where they had been organized and proselytized by an ex-priest named Menno Simons (who gave them his name, the Mennonites). They were offered a sanctuary in Pennsylvania by William Penn himself, and they settled at Germantown, near Philadelphia. The Mennonites soon spread throughout what was to become the United States and Canada, where they quickly broke into separate groups. Some preferred a more contemporary approach to life and theological beliefs; others favored a more rigid approach. A return to "primitive Christianity" was an ideal for many. Among the incoming Mennonites was a sect called the Amish, who took their name from Jacob Amman, a Swiss Mennonite bishop. There were also the Hutterites, named after Jakob Hutter, a Swiss Anabaptist.

The immigrating Germans included people known as the Brethren, a sect once Lutheran that dissented because its members found the new mother church to be "barren." They had derived doctrines from earlier dissenters known as the Pietists, and, like many of the left-wing peoples of the Reformation, sought to take the New Testament literally. They tried to put its teachings, down to the last mundane detail, into their daily lives. In common with

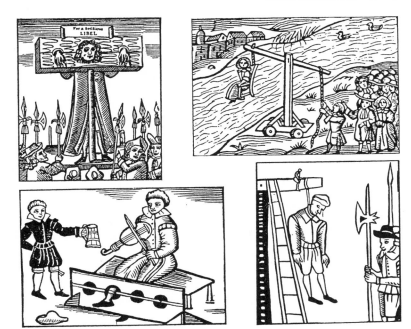

Harsh punishments for religious dissenters in Europe forced thousands of them to flee to the New World. The crushing of the Anabaptist peasants on the Continent and cruel measures against such groups as the Diggers, Ranters, Levellers, and Quakers—men possessed with the dual vision of the Holy Spirit and a better world on earth—uprooted society. Of all the English dissidents, the Pilgrims and the Puritans were easiest able to migrate to America, where in turn they applied equally brutal measures to other Christian religious dissenters.

many others, they dressed in the simplest of clothing, stood apart from amusements, refused military service, and would not engage in lawsuits. The Brethren are more often called Dunkers and Dunkards because they practiced total immersion in baptizing. Even here there was disagreement, however. There was argument over whether the baptized should be bent backward into the water, or forward, and immersed once or thrice. The latter practice was known as trine baptism, for it invoked one of the Trinity with each dousing.

Such sects are not only interesting but important. Though their direct influence on American religious life was peripheral, they still mirrored themes, ideas, theology, and practices which went back to the earliest days of Christianity. Their doctrines were borrowed or "discovered" anew by others, and they exist today as sound and touching vestiges of a religious fervor that literally shook a continent. Some of their offspring played pioneer roles, important for a decade and then forgotten, like Daniel Boone's footsteps in a forest path.

Under the direction of Johannes Kelpius, some of the immigrant Pietists broke off in the late seventeenth century to found a community in Pennsylvania called the Woman in the Wilderness because, as millennialists, they believed that Christ would appear in the wilderness, and the Church was symbolized as woman. For a while the group also was known as "The Contented of the God-Loving Soul." Kelpius practiced a mixture of Germanic paganism and magic, Rosicrucianism and Pietism, and preached communism, celibacy, and abstinence from alcohol. The community eventually failed. Another movement of more lasting importance was the Dunker offspring, the Seventh Day Baptists, German. (They are not to be confused with the Seventh Day Baptists founded by English-speaking immigrants.) The German sect owes its origin to the efforts of Peter Becker, who established the church in 1728. Becker was noted as a mystic, and he was unable to keep the more pious of his followers with him. Four years after the founding of the sect, Conrad Beissel decided that Becker was too worldly, and he moved deep into the Pennsylvania forest to establish Ephrata (an alternate name for Bethlehem). Beissel called his people, limited to forty (for that was a mystical number), the Spiritual Order of the Solitary. They were millennialists, practiced celibacy (men and women were segregated), and communism, and they observed the Sabbath on Saturday. Austerity was the guide: Men and women alike wore coarse woolen habits, slept on planks with stones for pillows, and lived on gruel with dry wheat bread. All looked emaciated. Still, they were famous for their beautiful music and literary output. Beissel was the author of the then-famous works the *Godly Chants of Love* and the *Ninety-nine Mystical Sentences*. Despite the many difficulties, the community continually attracted converts and, as late as 1950, could still report one hundred and fifty members in three churches.

Many of the ancient, so-called heretical sects of Europe owed their origins to primitive Gnostic churches that had their antecedents in pre-Christian Iran, Greece, and Egypt. Gnosticism is a complex subject. Briefly, Gnostics believed that under a One Supreme Deity (who was thought to be aloof from the affairs of the world and inactive after its creation) two forces controlled mankind, one good, one evil. In Christian as well as pagan Gnostic sects, there were lesser powers, various ranks of angels reminiscent of some huge governmental bureaucracy which played a part in running the world. Man's constant struggle was to overcome evil and practice good; evil existed so that good could triumph. For many of the Gnostic-inspired churches, sex was an evil, and thus marriage was proscribed. The established churches—Catholic, Orthodox, and, later, Protestant—took a more balanced view of marriage and sex. Thus the Waldensians, Bulgari, Cathars, and others with Gnostic antecedents were considered heretical and were much persecuted.

In the New World, Gnostic ideas could freely develop in the general toleration and openness of the frontier. A typical example was the church called the Two-Seed-in-the-Spirit Predestinarian Baptists founded by Elder Daniel Parker around 1820. Parker's theme of the Two Seeds is essentially Gnostic. Said Parker: Two seeds entered the life stream of humanity in the Garden of Eden. God planted a good seed and the devil, a bad seed. Since then the conflict has persisted in the souls of mankind. Every baby is born with one seed or the other, and nothing can be done to change his or her predestined life. Thus missions are useless, for the seed, good or bad, already exists in the spirit and cannot be changed. God needs no "new-fangled" help such as missions, nor does He need the corrupting influence of higher learning to advance the Gospel in the world. Parker said there should be no paid ministry, since "Christ came to save sinners, and He finished His work." For half a century Parker's doctrines influenced southern Baptists, but today his sect has virtually disappeared.

RELIGIOUS REBELLIONS IN ENGLAND

Since early in the seventeenth century, England had been the scene of great religious and political upheaval. Each rebellion helped to intensify the other. "Hatreds were intense and persecutions cruel and bitter, until men's minds and bodies gave way under the strain," said one witness. "The air was thick with reports of prophecies and miracles," wrote a historian. And, "There were men of all parties who lived on the border land between sanity and insanity."

The scene was one of long-continued tensions: Estates and lands were confiscated by the crown, ruining families; civil and religious dissenters were imprisoned under frightful conditions, with insufficient food, and suffered brutal treatment. In the numerous dissenting religious sects and even in the Established Church, believers began to lay claim to supernatural powers. Among the newer groups, prophecy, miracle-working, hypnotism and convulsive ecstacy, often to the edge of insanity, were but part of doctrine and ritual. Such sects as the Ranters and the Fifth Monarchy Men were notorious for their extravagances. About 1650, in the chaotic period following England's Civil War and the execution of Charles I by Oliver Cromwell, a group of dissenters thought the time was ripe for the Fifth Monarchy foretold in the prophecies of Daniel. Jesus would come down to earth and reign a thousand years; the sect believed the Lord would reign visibly on earth. In 1657, the Fifth Monarchy people asserted that Christ had indeed come, but for the moment He was unseen by the human eye. They formed a plot—or were accused of one—to kill Cromwell. Four years later they actually gathered the strength, pitiful in retrospect, to start an insurrection. They paraded through the streets of London with a banner showing a lion and claimed that Jesus was invisibly by their side. With King Jesus at their head, in person though unseen, they had the faith and the courage to declare that they were invulnerable and invincible. But the government forces shot them down. The Fifth Monarchy Men, relying upon divine intervention for protection, refused to heed the call to surrender. They fought to the death in the imminent expectation of the help of the Lord's mighty arm. The handful of survivors was tried and executed.

About the same time the equally apocalyptic sect of the Ranters seized the imagination of many of England's poor and despised. The Ranters were a chaotic and ill-defined sect, spiritualistic and individualistic. They were "antinomian," that is, they believed that nothing was sin except what each man believed to be sin. They tried to follow the practices and principles of the Primitive Church, and put much emphasis on psychic phenomena. The more orthodox Christians regarded them with horror.

One of the Ranter leaders claimed to be the incarnation of the biblical prophet Melchezidek, and even declared his own divinity. The new Melchezidek stated that certain persons then alive were Cain, Judas, Jeremiah, and other Old Testament figures whom he had raised from the dead. The people so-named stoutly affirmed the truth of Melchezidek's claims. Others among the Ranters asserted that the prophet had worked miracles and could produce lights and apparitions in the dark. The seventeenth-century Quaker apologist Robert Barclay believed that all the evidence "supports the view that these persons were mad, and had a singular power of producing a kind of sympathetic madness or temporary aberration of intellect in others."

Among the exiled French Protestants who reached England early in the eighteenth century, there was a group known as the Camisards, who showed forms of belief and practice that resembled those of the Fifth Monarchy Men and the Ranters. So extreme were the Camisards, that even in France they had been forced to live in seclusion in remote areas. The French prophets, said a historian, "carried with them the disease, both of mind and body, which their long sufferings had produced." Their meetings were marked "by such extravagance of convulsion and trance performance that they became the wonder of the ignorant and the scandal of the more intelligent classes. . . . They had visions and trances and were subject to violent agitations of body. Men and women, and even little children, were so exercised that spectators were struck with great wonder and astonishment."

The Methodist John Wesley (whose own people were then prone to highly emotional fits of weeping, dancing, crying out, and fainting from religious ecstasy) reported that when he visited one of the French prophets, the man suddenly fell into a fit and began to gobble like a turkey. However, Wesley was able to exorcize the victim, who told him that he had been possessed by Satan. On another occasion Wesley and some fellow Methodists visited a young woman who belonged to a prophets' church. Wesley wanted to know if the spirits that the prophets spoke to came from God. The woman went into a typical trance.

Presently she leaned back in her chair and had strong workings in her breast and uttered deep sighs [said Wesley]. Her head and hands and by turns every part of her body were affected with convulsive motions. This continued about ten minutes. Then she began to speak with a clear, strong voice, but so interrupted with the workings, sighings, and contortions of her body that she seldom brought forth half a sentence together. What she said was chiefly in spiritual words, and all as in the person of God, as if it were the language of immediate inspiration.

About 1740, the Jumpers, a sect quite similar in behavior, arose in Wales. They occupied a minor place in religious history, and are remembered mainly for their acts, which found parallel expression in other small churches. Wesley described them:

After the preaching was over anyone who pleased gave out a verse of a hymn, and this they sang over and over again, with all their might and main, thirty or forty times, till some of them worked themselves into a sort of drunkenness or madness; they were then violently agitated, and leaped up and down in all manner of postures frequently for hours together.

The Jumpers had a large following. One contemporary reported that he had seen as many as ten thousand of them "shouting out in the midst of the sermon and ready to leap for joy." Extreme as the Fifth Monarchy Men, the Ranters, and Jumpers seemed, they were but the antecedents of similar sects that would appear in America.

Many of the dissidents—poor, distraught people ravaged

by social conditions and religious doctrines of strange natures—
were deported to, or migrated to, the middle and southern Atlantic
coast of North America. The religions that developed in the areas
that came to be called the Deep South varied markedly in spirit,
intensity, and outlook from those of New England, already settled
for half a century.

THE NEW ENGLAND DOMINATION

In the long and exuberant history of America, it was the Puritan
and Pilgrim New Englanders, not the Anabaptist Germans, who
from the earliest times shaped much of American religious life,
and produced that peculiarly intense concept known as the Protestant Ethic, in which success in business was taken as a sign of
God's blessing bestowed upon the individual.

When the Pilgrims set sail for the New World in September 1620, after some seventeen years of exile in the Netherlands,
they were seeking to found a land where the "Earthly Jerusalem"
could be established. They had an apocalyptic vision of a New Zion
where they could worship God in their own theocracy. Soon after
them came other dissident Englishmen, the Puritans, closely allied
in thought and religious principles. The Puritans found the Church
of England, the product of Henry the Eighth's reformation, too
much like the Roman Catholic Church against which half of Europe had rebelled. What the immigrants wanted was a self-govern-
ing church of "visible saints"—themselves—which purified Christianity of all papist ties and influences and restored it to the clarity
and democracy of the Primitive Church of the first three centuries.

Soon Pilgrims and Puritans became as one, for their vision
was virtually identical. They believed their purity of purpose was
threatened by other newly arrived religious refugees, notably the
Quakers, whom they persecuted with a godly fury to the point of
death. Many of the newcomers suffered martyrdoms as tragic as
those of the religious wars they had tried to escape. The visible
saints believed that in their vision of the New Jerusalem they had
the right to annihilate heretics and sinners who did not fit into the
divine plan as they interpreted it. They felt particularly blessed, for

at their feet was a fertile land, seized from nonbelieving aborigines, the American Indians, for the sole purpose of establishing the Lord's domain on earth. It was this mystical sense that the hand of the Almighty was guiding and protecting them that enthused the Pilgrims and Puritans. It is a theme which can be found over and over again in the many sects that were to flower on American soil.

AMERICA

Out of the Pilgrims and Puritans came Congregationalism, a movement of virtually independent local churches—congregations that ruled with iron hands and persecuted sinners and dissenters with a wrath Jehovah Himself, in the most ferocious of Old Testament passages, could not equal. It was a stern, harsh, demanding deity whom they served. There was no room for pleasure, none for joy and play. Sex, even between husband and wife, was considered a temptation of the devil. Children (there were often many; the famous divine, Cotton Mather, had fifteen) were believed to be in a state of natural evil. Their will had to be broken before they could turn to the "love" of the Lord. Such attitudes produced either bigots or rebels, and both became abundant in New England.

Whatever faulty interpretations of Scripture they might have had, the Congregationalists had some redeeming qualities, at least in the abstract. They established democratic, independent governments in both churches and state for those who belonged to the group. Just who were truly members and who were not was a problem that constantly vexed the early Congregationalists. Almost all of the first settlers were united in purpose, principle, and belief. The difficulty came with succeeding generations. Many of the children, grandchildren, and so on found their elders' rule and fervor stultifying, to say the least. Those who could not adjust, or suffer and conform in silence, left. The westward migration of New Englanders was often sparked by people, especially the youth, who could not bear the continually oppressive atmosphere of Congregationalism, with its doctrines of salvation for the few and damnation for the many. This doctrine met a severe challenge in 1734 when the New England divine, Jonathan Edwards, in a sermon at Enfield, Connecticut, preached on justification—salvation—by faith alone. He said *all* who believed could be saved rather than just the certain few graced by God's selective will. The reaction that followed was known as the Great Awakening. It touched off a religious, theosophical, and philosophical debate that shook New England, upset the staid Congregationalists, affected the other churches, notably the Baptists, and gave birth to numerous new sects and splinter groups.

Even those who remained within the weakening orbit of strict Congregationalism and other Protestant faiths expressed opposition in subtle ways or even threw out orthodoxy wholesale. About the time of the American Revolution, the Unitarians dealt a severe blow to Congregationalism. The radical political doctrines of America's Founding Fathers had their echo in religion. Unitarianism rejected the hard and fast trinitarian beliefs of older churches, and relegated Jesus—to others the Son of God and divine—to the position of a human being of exceptional character. It also denied the Congregationalists' doctrine of salvation for the elect, and claimed that *all* would ultimately be saved. It was a belief already mirrored in the concept that all men were equal, as the new nation claimed.

The flush of enthusiasm for God's kingdom on earth, the temporal Jerusalem, was waning in New England. New beliefs spread rapidly, helped in part by increasing literacy, in part by the openness and freedom of American life, and by the opportunity to strike out for new lands if conditions at home were too oppressive. Intellectual curiosity helped bring about new doctrines. Many of the nineteenth-century Bostonians picked up a flavoring of Oriental mysticism (there were many Eastern influences then as the result of the China clipper trade) and shunned the rigors of the past in favor of intellectualism, optimism, "progress," and commercial acumen.

Around 1820, William Ellery Channing discovered that the human heart was not a refuge for total depravity as his Congregationalist forebears had taught. Instead it was a center for the natural loveliness which was a proof of God's grace. This theme was the basis for the Transcendentalist movement, which offered a new hope for sinful man. Sixteen years later the young poet Ralph Waldo Emerson asked why one should look to the past for authority, when "the sun shines today also." He stated that man's supposedly solid and intractable brute nature should be regarded as the fount of the "indwelling spirit" and a "projection of God in the unconscious." A year later, in an address at Harvard's divinity school, he said that "the need was never greater of new revelation than now."

The Boston intellectuals also found that the traditional image of God had changed. One of the most important of the Transcendentalists, Theodore Parker, prayed each Sunday for twenty years to "our Father and our Mother God." It was a concept that had been followed for centuries by peasants and workers.

Increasing literacy brought new attention to reading the Bible. Every man and woman, to say nothing of the children (who were often given the Book as a first reader), was able to make his or her own interpretation, something that had made the church of Rome uneasy in the Middle Ages, when it had restricted the sacred texts to the clergy and the educated for fear of erroneous conclusions about a complicated work. Many people could now note that the very first chapter of the book of Genesis had stated quite clearly and firmly that God was both male and female.

And God said, Let us make man in our image, after our likeness. . . . So God created man in his own image, in the image of God created he him; male and female created he them.

This reading was especially popular in some of the smaller sects of the eighteenth and nineteenth century. The Harmony Society, founded in 1814 on the east bank of the Wabash River in Illinois, by the German immigrant George Rapp, a former Lutheran, believed in the male-female interpretation. Rapp said that Adam was a "dual being, containing within his own person both the sexual elements" in literal confirmation of Genesis. Had Adam been content to remain in his original state, he would have increased without the help of a female, bringing forth new beings like himself to replenish the earth. But Adam became discontented and God separated from his body the female part and gave it to him according to his desires. The result was the fall of man. Conrad Beissel's Ephrata Community held similar views about the dual sex of the Creator, as did the Mormons of upper New York State. One of the most important interpreters of the dual sex of God was Mother Ann Lee, the founder of the Shakers, who was considered by her followers to be the Messiah in the form of a woman, a view she proposed herself to the faithful. Her official biography, prepared by the Shakers after her death, said in part:

As Father, *God is the infinite Fountain of intelligence, and the source of all power—"the Almighty, great and terrible in majesty"; "the high and lofty one, that inhabiteth eternity, whose name is Holy, dwelling in the high and holy place"; and "a consuming fire." But as Mother, "God is Love" and tenderness. If all the maternal affections of all female or bearing spirits in animated nature were combined together, and then concentrated in one individual female, that person would be but as a type or image of our Eternal Heavenly Mother.*

To the Shakers, Ann Lee was, of course, that Eternal Heavenly Mother.

The New England widow, Mary Baker Eddy, raised herself virtually to the level of Christ. In a letter in 1910 she stated:

Jesus was called Christ, only in the sense that you say, a Godlike man. I am only a Godlike woman, God-anointed, and I have done a lot of work that none others could do.

Some of the Christian Science faithful placed Mrs. Eddy dangerously close to Christ, seeing her as the female of the Messiah. In the words of one of her personal staff, Irving C. Tomlinson, she was "the Comforter, which is the Holy Ghost . . . who shall teach you all things." Tomlinson, a spokesman for the Christian Scientists, saw Mrs. Eddy, not Jesus, in terms of the Second Coming.

The healing work of Christian Science which she has given the world provides unassailable evidence of her position as the revelator of the Christ, Truth, of our age.

Expectation of Christ's return was but a natural part of the religious fervor so rampant in this country in the past and prevalent even today, especially in the large area known as the Bible Belt.

Religion was once as much a part of life as work. With few outlets—such as today's movies, television, general literacy, easy transportation, and widespread mobility—religion was a necessity, like food or shelter. More, it was an entertainment and a passion. Church-going dominated the free hours, and when one was not in church, singing or listening to hours-long sermons delivered by preachers noted for their flamboyance as well as their doctrines, one spent leisure time discussing the relative merits of Baptists over Methodists, or Presbyterians over Mormons and Shakers, or analyzing the reverend so-and-so's latest exhortation from the pulpit.

Religious fervor attained such heights of extremism that central New York State, the home of dozens of shades of doctrines carried in by ex-New Englanders, and the home of the Mormons, was known as "the burned-over area." Religious battles there struck fire not only in the souls of the faithful, but in a few of the churches belonging to opposition faiths. This religious ecstacy touched both the newly settled whites and the scattered and oppressed tribes of the Iroquois League. Parallel to the whites, the Indians of New York State experienced a religious awakening, expressed in the Good Message of the Seneca prophet, Handsome Lake.

In fact, what the whites did, or did not do, either in terms of settling the land or proclaiming their religion, had a profound effect upon the two subjected races of North America, the Indians and the black slaves. When the whites advanced westward, they pushed the Indians out of the forests, savannahs, and delta lands and from the Atlantic coastal strip. And as the whites imported slaves, they stripped them not only of their freedom but of their religion as well, forcing a simplified Christianity upon the blacks in place of the Islam and animism they had practiced in Africa. Reactions were to set in among both Indians and blacks. At first the Indians were pushed only across the Mississippi, in a manner partially deliberate and planned, partially at random. Even with the East cleared, the whites wanted further Indian lands. By the middle of the nineteenth century, except for those tribes that were able to escape the massive dragnets of the federal government or the random attacks by white settlers, the Indians from all over America were forced into what might be called a huge concentration camp, known as the Oklahoma Territory. There were Caddos from the Louisiana swamps, Delawares from Pennsylvania and New Jersey, Sioux from Minnesota and the Great Lakes, Cherokees from the Carolinas, Nez Percés from the tall forests of Oregon. There were tribes by the dozens from all types of environments, jammed together on the dusty, windy plains, their natural age-old forms of life destroyed, their hunting grounds but a distant memory, and their women and children dying of disease and hunger. Tragedy befell the warriors, men in the grip of demon fire water, the white man's panacea for keeping brave men docile. At the nadir of their misery, the Indians were awakened by a series of messiahs who could at least offer hope if little else.

Though the Indians could select what they chose of the white religion—they could note that Jesus was a white man killed by white men—the blacks were in a more precarious condition. As slaves they had no choice but to adopt the faiths of their masters. Many objected to the fact that God was white, but they kept their opinions to themselves. That many blacks became Christians of the best and most noble type is clear. Others, however, were restless and unhappy because the southern churches were generally segregated on a local, regional, and even a national level. Before the eyes of an all-loving white Lord, blacks were not worthy. Even before the Civil War, black freemen agitated for a return to Africa in movements that were part nationalistic, part religious, and ringing with the desperate cry that blacks must emigrate or perish. Such movements never came to fruition. Other forms of dissident action arose. Blacks took up Holiness and Pentecostalism with a fervor that put them in the fore of these more democratic movements.

Still other blacks turned to the various black messiahs, who preached special forms of black Christianity to impoverished ex-slaves and their children. The shadowy, flamboyant characters like Sweet Daddy Grace and Father Divine exploited their gullible faithful, lived in luxury, kept harems (Father Divine was notorious for his Rosebuds and his polygamous marriages), and managed quite well in the early decades of this century. But more substantial movements also arose, in particular the once-controversial sect known as the Muslims.

REVIVALISM

One can hardly question the explosive energy of the people who founded America. It was often admirable and creative, and it certainly produced a new man on the historical scene. After the Revolutionary War ended in 1789, the flow of people into the western areas became a stampede. Affected were the lands that came to be known as Kentucky, Ohio, Tennessee, Indiana, Illinois, and the Deep South (Alabama and Mississippi in particular). The old frontiers of New England and upper New York State gave way to new frontiers, requiring people of steel, with iron nerves, raw courage, unmitigated strength, hatred of the savages, and above all, a sense of destiny. As it was with the early settlers of New England and the Atlantic coast, it was primarily the young who ventured into new lands, against hostile and increasingly frustrated Indians.

Many of the settlers were unchurched, or had left their church affiliations behind. To reach the pioneer adventurers, the more nonconformist churches, especially the Presbyterians and Methodists, began to send out missionaries. The means of reaching the masses of people were the camp meeting and the revival. The technique had developed in the highly sophisticated atmosphere of Yale University, where "free-thinking" among the students had alarmed the administration. In 1802, a series of sermons by Yale's president, Timothy Dwight, brought an estimated one-third of the students back to orthodox views. Similar missions in other parts of New England and western New York State, still a raw frontier, had equally good results. People turned out by the hundreds and even the thousands to hear preachers thunder on about God and heaven and hell and call for repentance. The success of the eastern revivalists encouraged churchmen to head for the wilderness with its random hordes awaiting salvation. But where the East had shown a certain amount of civilized good taste, of restraint and good breeding, the West exhibited high emotion and the undisciplined fervor of an eager populace, a moving, floating people starved for any kind of message. Living often by wit alone, or trying to settle on land that still had to be cleared of both timber and Indians before it could be farmed, most of the early populace was, as one historian commented, "unusually rough, turbulent and unlettered." Many of the settlers had come from across the Appalachian chain, that long, rough, mountainous strip that runs from New York State into the South, an area where life had been harsh and deprived. The western migrants could be described, as one man was, as "an honest Georgian" on his way West, who "preferred his whiskey straight and his politics and religion hot."

Hot religion it was, of a fiery nature that promised the burning flames of hell to the sinner and the cooling waters of God's loving grace to the repentant. The wilderness was a land of extremes, and in the camp meetings the preachers and ministers could promise only extremes to the men and women of the frontiers. Ministers of different churches preached, stormed, and promised salvation, fighting for the souls of sinners and the faith of the saved. One of the most famous of the early nineteenth-century camp meetings was at Logan County in Kentucky, on the edge of the Tennessee border, a wild, remote, vicious spot. The area was described by the Methodist revivalist minister Peter Cartwright as "Rogue's Harbor," because it was a sanctuary for horse thieves, desperadoes, and runaways. The meeting came down to a battle over souls between Methodists and Presbyterians, with a Methodist minister, John McGee, gaining converts faster than the more staid Presbyterians. After three days of wild preaching, in which the people were very much worked up, McGee aroused and exhorted them to "let the Lord Omnipotent reign in their hearts." When one woman "shouted" for mercy, many in the crowd became agitated.

Several spoke to me [wrote McGee later]: "You know these people. Presbyterians are much for order, they will not bear this confusion. Go back and be quiet." I turned to go back and was nearly falling, [but] the power of God was strong upon me. I turned again, and losing sight of fear of man, I went through the house shouting and exhorting with all possible ecstacy and energy.

But the tide was turned in favor of the usually sedate Presbyterians, led by James McGready, noted for his fiery sermons. He wrote afterward that when he was finished preaching, the most notorious, profane swearers and Sabbath-breakers were "pricked to the heart" and many cried out, "What shall we do to be saved?" McGee reported that the ground was "covered by the slain in God" and "their screams for mercy pierced the heavens."

The success of this meeting led to numerous others. People traveled as far as a hundred miles, a considerable distance at that time, to join the multitudes begging for salvation. Crowds of ten thousand were estimated at one revival in Lexington, Kentucky. At a famous meeting in 1801 at nearby Cane Ridge, twenty-five thousand were present, an event that some people called "the greatest outpouring of the Spirit since Pentecost." Participants all later said that Cane Ridge challenged their descriptive powers. Rampant emotionalism and bodily agitation were the keynotes.

A later historian wrote:

With the traditional slow cycle of guilt, despair, hope, and assurance being compressed into a few days or even hours, the emotional stress was agonizingly intensified and it cut deep into normal restraint. Not only were there outbursts of weeping and shouts of joy, but frequently in the frenzied excitement of the moment, men and women were suddenly swept into physical "exercises"— falling, running, jumping, jerking—which were attributed to the smiting power of the Holy Spirit.

A Shaker named Evans, who was on a proselytizing mission to the area on behalf of his own people, reported that the crowds of Methodists and Presbyterians at the meetings were "greatly exercised in dreams, revelations, and the spirit of prophecy. In these gifts of the spirit they saw and testified that the great day of God was at hand, that Christ was about to set up His Kingdom on earth, and that this very work would terminate in the full manifestation of the latter day of glory."

The usual "rolls, jerks, and barks" peculiar to those seized by the Spirit were manifested. Evans continues:

The people remained on the ground day and night, listening to the most exciting sermons, and engaging in a mode of worship which consisted in alternate crying, laughing, singing, and shouting, accompanied with gesticulations of almost extraordinary character. Often there would be an unusual outcry; some bursting forth into loud ejaculations of thanksgiving; others exhorting their careless friends to "turn to the Lord"; some struck with terror, and hastening to escape; others trembling, weeping, and swooning away, till every appearance of life was gone, and the extremities of the body assumed the coldness of a corpse. At one meeting not less than a thousand persons fell to the ground, apparently without sense or motion. It was common to see them shed tears plentifully about an hour before they fell. They were then seized with a general tremor, and sometimes they uttered one or two piercing shrieks in the moment of falling. This latter phenomenon was common to both sexes, to all ages, and to all sorts of characters.

Evans had noted the expectation of the Second Coming of Jesus among the revivalists. His own people, the Shakers, already had seen the Second Coming in the form of a woman, their founder Mother Ann Lee.

This kind of hot-spirited evangelism, with its millennial hopes and its mystical fervor, its seizures "in the Spirit," continued throughout the century, and is just as much alive today. Once the revival was soundly established in the national life, evangelists by the hundreds, if not the thousands, traveled America. One of the greatest of the nineteenth century was the Massachusetts-born farm boy, Dwight Lyman Moody. While working as a shoe salesman in Boston, Moody, aged nineteen, had a conversion, "accepted

Christ," and was off on a career of bringing the message of salvation to the world. He moved to Chicago, where he joined the Plymouth Congregational Church, a conservative, Bible-centered, millennial organization. Moody began to take street children, drifters, and alcoholics to services, and he tried preaching. In 1863, with the help of some wealthy businessmen, he formed the independent, nondenominational Illinois Street Church. He also became influential in the YMCA. In 1872, while in England on business for the Y, he was asked to preach, which he did with remarkable success. In company with another American evangelist, Ira David Sankey, Moody toured England for three years, preaching the Second Coming and salvation for all. Some four million people were estimated to have heard him.

Back in America, he held evangelistic rallies in big cities from coast to coast with equal success. His message was simple: God's saving act for mankind was in Jesus Christ, and God's one goal was the conversion and salvation of the sinner—that is, of all mankind. Sinners and saved flocked by the millions to hear this country boy tell the cities of heaven and hell and salvation. One religious historian wrote:

Moody made it clear what he had known all along: The American-born, middle-class urbanite of his day was still a villager under the skin. Using the methods and money of big business, Moody reconciled the city and the old-time religion to each other.

After Moody retired in 1892, evangelism continued unabated, but few major figures arose to fill his shoes and his pulpit. J. Wilbur Chapman, Reuben A. Torrey, Samuel Porter Jones, and Benjamin Fay Mills were the best known of his successors. Jones, like Moody a country boy, preached the standards of rural, conservative, church-going Georgia as the guide for big-city life. Mills was skilled in applying the latest techniques of business to evangelism. Religious road shows were by now a basic ingredient of the American scene. In 1911, a survey totaled six hundred and fifty active and twelve hundred part-time evangelists. In the years between the taking of the survey and the end of World War I in 1918, Americans were found to have attended thirty-five thousand revival meetings, some of them lasting days and even weeks. And evangelism, adding to its techniques, had entered still another phase, borrowing not only from the best of big business but also from Hollywood. The fiery Red "Gypsy" Smith combined theatrical tricks with religion, and boasted to his sponsors that he could produce converts for "$4.92 apiece."

But the best known of all, a man whose name is still something of a household word for what is good and bad in evangelism, was Billy Sunday. Like many of the other evangelists, Sunday was a farm boy. He was born in Iowa, and at the age of twenty he became a big-league baseball player, playing for three years as an outfielder for the Chicago White-Stockings. In 1886, aged twenty-three, he was "converted," and almost immediately went into preaching. Never had America seen religion delivered in such a guise. Sunday was odd enough and blatant enough to bring forth satire and scorn, but millions followed him faithfully. The effect he had was profound. He was a fundamentalist in belief, who denounced not only modern science but modern theology and social reform as well. He was agile in the pulpit, as if winding up for a pitch, and his language was coarse almost to the point of foulness. His sermons rushed out in a torrent of words, as he smashed furniture and partially undressed himself. He could denounce the "bastard theory of evolution," and the "deodorized and disinfected sermons" of "hireling ministers" (that is, theological and social liberals). He made famous the phrase "muscular Christianity," which equated salvation with decency and manliness. The ideal Christian was "the man who has real, rich, red blood in his veins instead of pink tea and ice water." And the ideal Christian was also the fighting man of God, not a "hog-jowled, weasel-eyed, sponge-columned, mushy-fisted, jelly-spined, pussy-footing, four-flushing, charlotte-russe." To Sunday, "Christianity and patriotism are synonymous terms," just as "hell and traitors are synonymous." During World War I he blamed atrocities attributed to the German army to the baneful influence of modern biblical scholarship upon the German people.

When Sunday died in 1935, his antics had done much to

discredit revivalism. It was not until the more middle-of-the-road and less flamboyant preachings of such people as Billy Graham, Oral Roberts, Jimmy Swaggart, and even the Roman Catholic Fulton J. Sheehan—all of whom appeared after the second world war—that revivalism and evangelism were given a better tone and a more respectable name.

For the lonely, bearded saint who sets up stones for Jesus and gives out peanut butter and jelly sandwiches in His name; the faithful drinking at God's Well; for those of the many sects, churches, and cults who daily await the Lord's imminent arrival; for the fiery Witnesses who carry Jehovah's name from door to door; for those who *know* that the saved can be found only among the faithful who worship on Saturday and not Sunday—for all these and millions more, religion is the only thing that matters in life. All are God-obsessed.

It is with the experiences of the Shakers' Mother Ann Lee that this book truly begins. In her teachings are ancient themes that engaged Christianity over the centuries: the mystical fervor that produced such sects as the Ranters and Jumpers, that proclaimed the Second Coming of the Lord (in this case in the body of a woman), and the imminence of the millennium, along with the extreme notions about sex that set heretics, nonconformists, and dissenters aside from the mainstream of Christianity.

2

THE SHAKERS

REMARKABLE WOMAN.
She was an immigrant mystic, Ann Lee. She was uneducated, illiterate, given to trances, fits of religious ecstacy,
visions, dancing on the Sabbath, and speaking in strange tongues
in the midst of church services. Virtually an outcast in England,
where she was born and raised, she was to make a profound
impression on American religion and upon her adopted country's
artistic life. Her imprint was visionary and strange, practical, inventive, beautiful, and communitarian. The sect she founded, the
Shakers, formally known as the United Society of Believers in
Christ's Second Coming, is today remembered largely for its super-
ficialities and secondary qualities, not its essentials. Still the Believ-

ers (as they liked to call themselves) are honored for the purity of their insights and the effectiveness with which they expressed them.

Ann Lee was born in Manchester, England. Her father was a poor blacksmith. When she was in her twenties, he married her off, apparently against her will, to another blacksmith. Ann seems to have feared sex. She entered into the marriage primarily because of parental desires and, possibly, to escape her own miserable life as a millhand and as a cook in a poorhouse. Her name would have been lost in time and history along with those of millions of other poor, brutalized working people, except for the fact that she entered wholeheartedly into the religious ferment of her age, going beyond it into the creative and positive movement called the Shakers.

Ann Lee's century, the eighteenth, experienced the climax of the religious fervor, dissent and conflict, and excitement of the previous periods in England. It benefited from the nonconforming sects—Puritans, Methodists, Presbyterians, Baptists (and Anabaptists), Quakers—and other dissenters that had challenged the Established Church, the Church of England. The formalism of the state church, with its priesthood, liturgies, vestments, ceremonies, holy days, dogmas, and creeds, all vestiges of its former ties with the Roman Catholic Church, was rejected in favor of simpler yet more evangelical ways. A search for, or a return to, original forms of Christianity, supposedly more authentic, along with a reliance upon the workings of the Holy Spirit within the individual (the Inner Voice, or the Inner Light, as the Quakers called it), made "everyone a walking church and every heart God's altar and shrine." This was in sharp contrast to the elaborate formalism of the Established Church and its consecrated priesthood. Many of the English sects, especially the Quakers, refused to pay taxes, would not take oaths in court, were pacifists, claimed there was no distinction between classes (often all members, rich or poor, wore the same type of simple rough clothing), and even disowned the authority of the king in preference to God's direct rule.

The Quakers influenced many people. A group known as

the Shaking Quakers, led by a pair of ex-Quakers, James and Jane Wardley, both tailors, attracted Ann Lee. The Wardleys had been affected by the doctrines of a sect of French Protestant religious refugees, the Camisards, who had come to England in 1685 with other French "prophets" when religious toleration for non-Catholics ended in France. The Edict of Nantes, which allowed Protestants and others freedom of worship, had been revoked. Scattered groups of Camisards in the more tolerant atmosphere of England preached the approaching end of the world and the Second Coming of Jesus, and called for the sinful to amend their ways. The Camisards reported signs in the skies, heavenly lights and heavenly voices, and other supernatural events as proof of their divine guidance. They fasted and experienced trances, with much shaking of the head and limbs, under divine inspiration.

The Wardleys took Camisard beliefs a few steps further. They developed the doctrine that the Second Coming of Jesus would be in the form of a woman. They also claimed the Holy Spirit, whose presence and power gave them the ability to speak in strange tongues, heal the sick, and predict the future. The Wardleys believed in open public confession of sins, first for admission into their church and secondly for salvation. The more orthodox Quakers merely "quaked" in the presence of the Lord. The Wardleys and their followers danced and jumped to show their exuberance in Him. As with the earlier Ranters and Jumpers, the Shaking Quakers would begin their meetings in quiet and then enter into . . .

. . . a mightly trembling, under which they would express the indignation of God against all sins. At other times they were affected under the power of God, with a mighty shaking; and were occasionally exercised in singing, shouting, or walking about the floor, under the influence of spiritual signs, shoving each other about—or swiftly passing and repassing each other, like clouds by a mighty wind.

In common with other dissenters and nonconformists, the Wardleys were violently opposed to the established forms of religion:

The new heaven and the new earth prophesied of old is about to come. . . . And when Christ appears again, and the true church rises in full and transcendent glory, then all the anti-Christian denominations—the priests, the pope—will be swept away.

The brutal life of a working woman—her poor peasant body stunted by privation as a child, hardened by the long hours in the factory and the poorhouse, some strangely negative ideas about sex—and whatever else went into her character and life, led Ann Lee to search for a religious outlet. The Wardleys' Shaking Quakers fulfilled her needs. In 1758, aged twenty-two, Ann Lee joined their church. However, when two years later her father married her off to one Abraham Stanley, the ceremony was performed in the Anglican church.

Ann bore four children, all of whom died in infancy. She took the multiple tragedy as a sign that the Lord frowned upon the lust of the marital bed. The deaths of the children were, she believed, a judgment upon her "concupiscence." From then on, for fear of arousing the passions in her husband, she avoided their bed at night "as if it had been made of embers." Her main outlet—emotional, physical, religious—was in the Shaking Quakers. Her entire being was committed to the untrammeled expression of the Inner Search. Her life was fraught with religious excitement and emotion.

In their efforts to bring the public to the true Way to salvation, the Wardley sect seemed committed to antagonizing the authorities, religious or civil. On numerous occasions the members of the sect—especially Ann Lee—were imprisoned for activities considered blasphemous or a nuisance. Ann Lee was arrested several times—the details are not clear—on such charges as dancing in public and shouting on the Sabbath, both serious offenses. She was charged also with blasphemy. On several occasions she escaped death at the hands of mobs enraged at the public expression of her beliefs. In one instance, a man attacked her with a broom handle when she was sitting in a chair "singing by the power of God. . . . He then beat me over my face and nose with his staff till one end of it was much splintered." However she was saved. "I sensibly felt and saw the bright rays of the glory of God pass between my face and his staff, which shielded off the blows, so that he had to stop and call for drink." Again she was beaten with a broom staff, stoned, thrown from a window, tied and bound, left all night on the ice, clubbed, kicked, and abused. But often she was rescued from harm by "the presence of God"—and "my soul was filled with love."

On one occasion, she reported years later to her disciples, she confounded four Anglican clergymen by speaking in seventy-two tongues over a four-hour period "so perfectly that they flattered me with an offer to teach the languages." (In another version of the incident she spoke a mere twelve languages, including French, Hebrew, Greek, and Latin.)

In 1770—or 1773 (the sequence of events in her life in England is far from lucid)—she was arrested for disturbing an Anglican service by speaking out in tongues and making irreverent charges in a loud voice. The sentence was fourteen days imprisonment. Her stay in Manchester jail marked a turning point in her life. She experienced a series of visions, including "the vision of the very transgression of the first man and woman in the Garden of Eden, the cause wherein all mankind was lost and separated from God." She told her followers that Christ appeared to her, to offer comfort with His presence, and to command her to preach the Gospel of the stainless life. The spirit of Jesus so infused her that she could now believe that she was His special instrument. "It is not that I speak, it is the Christ who dwells in me," she told the world.

I converse with Christ. I feel his presence with me, as sensibly as I feel my hands together. . . . I have been walking fine vallies with Christ, as with a lover. . . . I am married to the Lord Jesus Christ. He is my head and my husband, and I have no other. I have walked, hand in hand, with him in heaven. . . . I feel the blood of Christ running through my soul and body, washing me; Him I do acknowledge as my head and Lord.

The purity of Christ—His freedom from sexual sins—became a

central doctrine for Ann Lee, along with confession of past transgressions.

A complete cross against the lust of generation, added to a full and explicit confession before witnesses of all the sins committed under its influence, is the only possible remedy and means of salvation.

Somewhere in this period Ann had been gradually assuming a more important role in the Wardleys' sect, replacing Mother Jane Wardley as the leader of the group. Upon her release from her last prison term, Ann Lee returned to the world with the message that "I am the Word." This meant that she was the feminine of the Christ, and that Mother Jane, being relegated to second place, became a "John the Baptist in the female line." With the power of "the light thereof, to search every heart and try every soul," Ann was now the "Mother of the new creation." She formally took the title of Mother, and all the Wardley group accepted her as leader. Doctrines became stricter during this period, with a special emphasis on purity.

The conversion of several wealthy, propertied men and their families gave the sect a sound financial basis. A number of members of Mother Ann's family, including her younger brother William, who had served as an officer of horse in the Oxford Blues, a regiment of the king's guard, helped strengthen the movement. One of the visions Mother Ann experienced—several times—was that of "chosen people" awaiting her in America. Her revelation was confirmed by a new member, James Whittaker, who received a vision of the new church as a large tree whose leaves "shone with such brightness, as made it appear like a burning torch." In the spring of 1774 the final decision to emigrate to the Americas was made, and preparations were worked out for the voyage to find the refuge in which the Second Coming could be realized and God's kingdom on earth be experienced.

THE SETTLEMENT

A small group of Shaking Quakers arrived in New York in August

1774. Along with Mother Ann there were seven others, including, strangely enough, her husband Abraham Stanley, who soon disappeared. The others were: her brother William; her niece Nancy; the young visionary James Whittaker, who seemed to have been brought up by Mother Ann and may have been a relative; and a well-off follower named John Hocknell, who financed the trip. Hocknell was accompanied by his son Richard, and there were two others, James Shepherd and Mary Partington.

The New World was in an upheaval. Trouble with the mother country was looming. The first armed clash between the American colonists had broken out in 1773 at Lexington and Concord after a group of Bostonians had dumped a load of English tea into the harbor as a protest against the high taxation imposed on the colonies. Soon the skirmishes erupted into a war and engulfed the entire eastern coast of North America as George Washington, a Virginian, was given charge of the scattered and unruly colonial troops. Meanwhile the small group of Shaking Quakers was dispersed as each member tried to survive in this unexpected turmoil. Mother Ann remained in New York City, at the time a large town of some fifteen thousand people.

In 1776—a fateful year in American history—Hocknell found and bought land in the tiny community of Niskeyuna in the township of Watervliet, near Albany, New York. Mother Ann was able to draw her scattered flock together, to settle and farm. Instead of each member living and working independently, as in Manchester, it now seemed wisest for all to live communally. This rudimentary settlement was the origin of the famous Shaker colonies, and it was the embodiment of a dream long held throughout Europe, the "perfect" Christian society, the New Jerusalem on earth, ruled not by men but by God Himself speaking directly to His chosen people through visions and inspiration. In the past all such attempts had sooner or later failed. Religious and civil authorities often believed the communes to be heretical and against the state; some groups' principles had not been properly defined; and many groups suffered from internal dissension. The New World, however, with its openness and freedom from social pressures, its riches in land and resources to be had for the taking (from non-Christian and therefore "savage" Indians), and its open spaces and isolation from others seemed to many visionary settlers to be ideal for such experiments. The Shakers were among the first, and the following century would see such settlements by the dozen. Though initially they clung together for their own good, Mother Ann and her people came to believe that a communal way of life was an example of Christian perfectionism.

Around the Shakers the war against England continued. The Hudson Valley in which they had settled was a constant battleground, from Manhattan up into Canada. There was much poverty, social unrest, and unemployment. Against this turmoil there was a mass, vast, popular interest in religion, a trend that was to mark the American scene for decades to come. New Lebanon, not far from Niskeyuna, became the battleground for an intense theological struggle between contending groups of Baptists. A new movement, the New Lights—also called the Separatists—had challenged the traditionalists, dubbed the Old Lights. The New Lights believed in good works and conditional salvation; the Old Lights held fast to the theme of salvation for the elect. It was a battle that later would continue not only among Baptists but Congregationalists and Methodists. Intense excitement filled the days and nights at New Lebanon and the nearby towns across the border in Massachussetts. Wild, exalted preaching, shouting, and screaming marked the evening revival meetings. "Free to speak or sing as the spirit gave utterance," the New Lights often expressed themselves with such exuberance that they were named the "Come-Outers" and "Merry Dancers." Some people experienced visions and uttered prophecies in trances. Men and women in their ecstacies of fervor fell to the ground "as if wounded in battle"—a phrase often applied to the participants of other, later revivals.

The hot debates between New Lights and Old Lights eventually calmed down, leaving members with wounded and impaired religious sensibilities. But the parties were unable to resolve their differences. Two disappointed New Light members, Talmadge Bishop and Reuben Wright, decided to go to the western wilderness to begin life afresh. They happened to pass the tiny Believer settlement at Niskeyuna, where they were invited to spend

Shaker dancing, once wild and exuberant, became more rigidly routinized as the brotherhood gained respectability. The Shakers believed that dancing was "the gift of God to the church," and that they had restored the ancient biblical practice of King David.

the night. Here they witnessed the strange ceremonies of Mother Ann's Shakers, the dancing, the singing, the clear-cut dedication to God. Moreover, Bishop and Wright learned that the Second Coming was present in the person of Mother Ann, and that the resurrection and the day of reckoning were already accomplished. The world would not end in a great cataclysm as others believed, but when each individual passed from worldly life into the true life of the spirit.

Heartened by the unexpected and forceful message, the two men abandoned their plans to go west, and returned to their homes, to tell of their discovery. Joseph Meacham, a leading Baptist minister and a force in the New Light Baptists at New Lebanon, was so impressed by what he learned from Bishop and Wright that he sent one of his most trusted associates to investigate Mother Ann's movement. The report was favorable, and Meacham himself went to Niskeyuna. The Shakers recorded an extensive conversation between Meacham and the Shakers, with young Whittaker doing most of the talking. A summary of the discussion came when Meacham asked if the Shakers were able to live without sin. Whittaker replied:

The Power of God, revealed in this day [that is, at the present time], does enable souls to cease from sin; and we have received that power; we have actually left off committing sin, and we live in daily obedience to the will of God.

This confrontation, with Meacham's immediate conversion, was the turning point in Believer history. Up to this time Mother Ann had gained but one convert, a local woman. Mother Ann had made a favorable impression on Meacham and he returned with many of his own people. The clarity of the Shaker doctrine and the unusual way in which they lived, the cool fervor of their beliefs, stressing the Power of God which enabled souls to exist without sin, the community's ability to live in daily obedience to Him—all these were powerful arguments for the soundness of their faith. But, the Shakers continually emphasized, their way could be achieved only by forsaking "the marriage of the flesh." It was a sacrifice many were willing to make. Though the local Congregationalists and Baptists were within the mainstream of Christian orthodoxy, there was an ancient undercurrent in their churches which denounced carnal thoughts and practices, even within marriage. It was but a short step for Meacham and the others to go over entirely to the Believers.

May 10, 1780, was a day celebrated as the "dark day" in the northeast. The sun did not appear, though there were no clouds, and the populace believed the day of judgment had at last arrived. Meacham and a number of his flock were formally received into the Shakers. Meacham's conversion, along with the reports of miraculous events at Niskeyuna—among them "healing and signs"—brought in more converts by the dozens, even though they had to renounce "the lust of the flesh, the lust of the eye, and the pride of life."

Shaker teachings on sex are firm:

The deceitful wantonness of both male and female brings distress and poverty, shame and disgrace upon families and individuals, and fills the earth with wretchedness and misery.
The marriage of the flesh is a covenant with death, and an agreement with hell. . . . If you want to marry, you may marry the Lord Jesus Christ.

Yet the converts continued to come. And hardly had the movement attained its first fame than it ran into trouble with the new Revolutionary government. The Shaker elders were British. They refused to support the new nation of the United States, not because of ties to the motherland, but because they were pacifists, against wars and against governments (though they obeyed the civil laws). Virtually all the elders, British-born, were arrested in July 1780, and imprisoned; the elders were soon released, but Mother Ann, sent to prison in Poughkeepsie because it was far from the British lines, was not given her freedom until December. By this time the Believers had achieved a fair measure of fame—or notoriety—for their beliefs. When Mother Ann set off on a two-year missionary tour of New England, she was already well known, infamous to some, to others a welcome messenger of the New Jerusalem.

With Mother Ann were some of her original group and a few new members. They met with mixed receptions. Fervent and sincere converts were made and kept, but at the same time the Shakers were accused of witchcraft and popery, the last charge because of their insistence on confession as a necessity for salvation. Mobs attacked them and ran them out of town. They were horsewhipped and beaten with rails. There were continued scenes of . . .

. . . cruelty and abuse; whipping with horsewhips, pounding, beating and bruising with clubs, collaring, pushing off from bridges, into the water and mud, searing the sisters' horses with a view to frightening the riders, and every kind of abuse they [the enemies of the Shakers] could invent without taking lives.

James Shepherd, one of the original members, was stripped and beaten, but he took the whipping as a saint and said, "Be of good cheer, brethren, for it is your heavenly Father's good pleasure to give you the kingdom." Even Mother Ann was not spared. In Petersham, Massachusetts, she was "shamefully and cruelly abused." A mob . . .

. . . seized her by the feet, and inhumanly dragged her, feet foremost, out of the house, and threw her into a sleigh, with as little ceremony as they would the dead carcass of a beast, and drove off, committing at the same time, acts of inhumanity and indecency which even savages would be ashamed of . . . [tearing] her clothes in a shameful manner. Their pretence was to find out whether she was a woman or not.

Strict though the Believers' doctrine was, and hostile as many of their hearers might be (even scurrilous pamphlets against them were published), they continued to make converts. A convert, John Cotton, tells how he was "sealed." The incident has a strong touch of the miraculous.

The power of God came upon me, filling my soul and controlling my whole being. It raised me from my chair and under its influence I turned around, swiftly, for the space of half an hour. The door of the house was open. I was whirled through the door-way into the yard among the stones and stumps, down to the shore of the Mascoma Lake, some rods distant. On reaching the shore of the lake that same power that led me to the water whirled me back again in like manner, and I found myself in the same chair that I had been taken from.

New settlements were founded throughout New England, all based on the same kind of rough communism that had begun at Niskeyuna. Possessions were pooled in common, if the owner felt free to do so, as a "joint interest." Members worked "for the good and benefit of the whole society." A free table was kept, open to all, to

Shaker and passerby alike, especially the poor. Everywhere Mother Ann announced that she was the Second Coming in person. She urged her listeners to celibacy. She did not forbid marriage, but thought it an imperfect state. Families which could not practice celibacy were able to join the community but remained in an outer circle of Believers. Ann was the "Second pillar of the Church of God," and the Shakers, as everyone knew them, were the forward troops, the intercessors whose examples in holiness and prayer would lead all into blessedness. They brought salvation to every individual, not to the elect, as the popular and all powerful Congregationalists, and some of the Baptists taught. Mother Ann enjoined public confession upon all as a necessity for salvation; and each member had to practice the twelve virtues and follow the four moral precepts. The Kingdom was literally at hand—Mother Ann was the visual proof. She was able to communicate with the dead, as were certain of her followers (this power died out in 1837, when people apparently lacked the sanctity for the gift).

A man named William Plumer, later governor of New Hampshire and a United States senator, described a meeting at Harvard, Massachusetts, in 1782:

About thirty of them assembled in a large room in a private house—the women in one end and the men in the other—for dancing. Some were past sixty years old. Some had their eyes steadily fixed upward, continually reaching out and drawing in their arms and lifting up first one foot, then the other, about four inches from the floor. Near the centre of the room stood two young women, one of them very handsome, who whirled round and round for the space of fifteen minutes, nearly as fast as the rim of a spinning-wheel in quick motion. . . . As soon as she left whirling she entered the dance, and danced gracefully. Sometimes one would pronounce with a loud voice, "Ho, ho," or "Love, love"—and then the whole ensembly vehemently clapped hands for a minute or two. At other times some were shaking and trembling, others singing words out of the Psalms in whining, canting tones (but not in rhythm), while others were speaking in what they called "the unknown tongue"— to me an unintelligible jargon, more gibberish and perfect non-

sense. At other times the whole assembly would shout as with one voice, with one accord. This exercise continued about an hour.

Similar accounts are found in many works of the period. Valentine Rathbun, who joined the Shakers and eventually left, gave a somewhat hostile report:

When they meet together for their worship, they fall a groaning and trembling, and everyone acts alone for himself; one will fall prostrate on the floor, another on his knees and his head in his hands; another will be muttering over articulate sounds, which neither they nor any body else understand. Some will be singing, each one his own tune; some without words, in an Indian tune, some sing jig tunes, some tunes of their own making, in an unknown mutter, which they call new tongues; some will be dancing, and others stand laughing, heartily and loudly; others will be drumming on the floor with their feet, as though a pair of drumsticks were beating a ruff on a drum-head; others will be agonizing, as though they were in great pain; others jumping up and down; others fluttering over somebody, and talking to them; others will be shooing and hissing evil spirits out of the house, till the different tunes, groaning, jumping, dancing, drumming, laughing, talking and fluttering, shooing and hissing, makes a perfect bedlam; this they call the worship of God.

ELDRESS LUCY TAKES CHARGE

Life had been hard for Mother Ann, and the rugged trip through New England, after years of privation and struggle, had worn her down. In July 1784, her younger brother William died, causing her much grief. Six weeks later, on September 8, she, too, passed away. The Believers spoke of her "departure." She was heard to say, "I see Brother William coming, in a golden chariot to take me home."

Mother Ann's "departure" shattered the community. Many people left for other sects, and the faithful were attacked by doubts. It was an act of faith that the New Jerusalem had already been proclaimed on earth. Leadership passed by common consent to John Whittaker, one of the original members. Whittaker, in three years of rule—a harsh and rigid one, from the criticism—still pulled the community together, and expanded it, sending out missionaries and commencing a program of building in the different centers of Shaker strength. When he died at the age of 36, in July 1787, he was mourned by the flock, despite his faults.

Whittaker's rule had been tremendously aided by two elders: an original member, Lucy Wright, and the convert from the New Light Baptists, Joseph Meacham. Upon Whittaker's death they took over. Meacham was the senior elder, and he led the Believers until his death in 1796. After that, Lucy Wright led the society for twenty-five years, helping give it the strength and prominence that marked it during Shakerism's best and most effective years. It was under her that Shaker communism developed its most sincere form. New communities were founded regularly. In 1794, the year of Meacham's rule, there were twelve communities, two in New York State, the others in New England. In 1805, under Eldress Lucy's charge, a concentrated missionary effort in the Midwest, then a frontier territory, brought large numbers of converts. By 1809, two communities had been founded in Kentucky and two in Ohio. The latter state saw another two Shaker centers soon added, and there was one in Indiana. Union Village in Ohio became the sect's largest foundation, with four thousand five hundred acres. The Shakers reached the peak of their growth in the two decades between 1830 and 1850, numbering nineteen communities (one as far away as Florida), with about six thousand members.

The Society had a strong missionary fervor from the first days. Members traveled thousands of miles on foot to speak and preach the message of God's immanence. A single Shaker converted some thousand settlers in the Ohio Valley beginning in 1801.

The message was simple: God's immanence was in the form of Ann, who expressed the dualism of God, both male and female "in our image." Jesus, the carpenter, born of a woman, incorporated the male manifestation of Christ, the Anointed One and the Primitive Church, while Mother Ann, daughter of an English blacksmith, expressed the female principle of Christ and the second Christian Church. Ancient Christian images were restated. Ann was the Bride ready for the Bridegroom. But the Shakers did not believe in the divinity of Jesus nor in the traditional Christian teaching of the Resurrection of the body. Salvation is here, at this moment, resurrection is now. "We have risen with Christ and travel with Him to the resurrection [that is, of the flesh]," said one of the first elders.

Because of their emphasis upon sex, even though they frowned upon it, the Believers were accused of debauchery and nudism. They were said to be "the principle enemies of America." The Wardleys' dancing, continued on this continent, became the mark of Shaker worship, though other sects then and later also used forms of dance and music in their ceremonies. Shaker dancing was a scandal to more straight-laced Protestants. "Bodily agitation" smacked of Roman Catholicism for no good reason, though the Shakers were distinctly anti-Catholic, believing as many others had for centuries, that the Roman Church was the Biblical Whore of Babylon. The Believer practice of confession, though public and not private as with the Catholics, also brought accusations of popery.

But such charges were part of the world's miscomprehension of the Shakers. They were on earth to do the work of God, which was to build His millennial church. Whatever they did, their simple and exuberant worship, as well as their daily lives, had to give proof to this work. They were excellent farmers, their methods widely admired, and their seeds, produced by some communities, were known as the best available. Their houses were models of excellent design and craftmanship, as was their furniture. It is this aspect of their lives which has carried their fame to the present, when their doctrines have long been forgotten but their excellent taste remembered and praised. Good design and good workmanship were as basic to the Shaker way of life as belief in Mother Ann as the Second Coming, and one might suggest that their adherence to celibacy was reflected in the stark, clean, graceful lines of their furniture. Beds, chairs, tables, utensils, and clothing were all made for simplicity, practicality, and economy of means. No article could be made, used, or sold which was "superfluously wrought."

Shaker taste, however, was not to the liking of the ordinary nineteenth-century citizen who admired bric-a-brac, knickknacks, doodads, and clutter, and who wallowed in ponderous chairs, thick, patterned carpets, heavy draperies, flowered wallpapers, and a jungle of curios and mementoes strewn about tables and sideboards. When Charles Dickens visited the Shaker community at Mount Lebanon, New York, in 1842, he wrote home: "We walked into a grim room, where several grim hats were hanging on grim pegs, and the time was grimly told by a grim clock." Today, bare white walls, bare floors, and slim tables and chairs prove to us that "Less is more," and that the Shakers had a special genius for living.

A more appreciative visitor, William Hepworth Dixon, followed Dickens to New Lebanon in 1869 and had a different reaction:

A bed stands in the corner, with sheets and pillows of spotless white. A table on which lie an English Bible, some few Shaker tracts, an inkstand, a paper-knife; four cane chairs, arranged by angles; a piece of carpet by the bedside; spittoon in one corner complete the furniture. A closet on one side of the room contains a second bed, a wash-stand, a jug of water, towels; and the whole apartment is light and airy, even for a frame house.

Simplicity was the result of Mother Ann's thinking about the nature of man. The Believers were not to produce anything which would "feed the pride and vanity of man." Moreover, "Buildings, moldings and cornices which are merely for fancy may not be made by Believers." She also said: "Put your hands to work and your hearts to God," and, "Clean your room well, for good spirits will not live long where there is dirt. There is no dirt in heaven." In explaining why frivolous and showy tastes for ornamentation were rejected by the Shakers, an elder said: "The divine man has no right to waste money upon what you would call beauty in his house or daily life, while there are people living in misery."

The emphasis on simplicity and cleanliness led to some basic utensils which soon became popular all over America. The flat straw broom is a Shaker invention, as is the clothespin. Shakers—clean to the point of fanaticism—made the first model of a washing machine. The insistence on good craftmanship for the honor of God was not carried out in a spirit of drudgery or compulsion. In fact, the worker was not to overwork himself. Work was to be carried on at a steady, peaceful rhythm. An elder said:

We are not called upon to labor to excel, or to be like the world; but to excel them in order, union, peace and in good works— works that are truly virtuous and useful to man in this life. . . . All work done or things made in the Church for their own use ought to be faithfully and well done but plain and without superfluity. All things ought to be made according to their order and use.

Thinking about work produced among the Shakers a number of maxims which have a very contemporary air. "Every force evolves a form" is one. Others sound more traditional:

Do be natural, a poor diamond is better than an imitation.
Do not be troubled because you have no great virtues. God made a million spears of grass where He made one tree.
Do be truthful; do avoid exaggeration; if you mean a mile, say a mile, and if you mean one, say one, and not a dozen.
Whatever is really useful is virtuous though it does not at first seem so.
Order is the creation of beauty. It is heaven's first law, and the protection of souls.

More mystical is:

Sincerity is the property of the universe.

Though the Shakers themselves, their friends and sympathizers, knew they were leading lives of honesty and probity, they had many enemies who did not understand. They were accused of sin and debauchery, of holding children prisoner, and even of castrating each other. In the early 1800s there was much mob violence against some of the communities. In 1819, there was an especially bitter attack on Union Village in Ohio, when five hundred armed men led a mob of a thousand against the settlement, demanding the release of orphaned children who had been sent to the Shakers. Previous to the attack, fences had been broken down, windows and doors smashed, horses disfigured, cattle released, and houses set on fire. But the Shakers held on, and the violence abated.

In 1837, a strange mystical wave seized the communities, starting at Niskeyuna and spreading to other villages. Young women began to experience visions, saw angels and took journeys to heavenly places under the guidance of spirits. This marked the beginning of a ten-year period known as Mother Ann's Second Appearance, or Mother Ann's Work. Sometimes the women would fall to the floor in a trance, speak in strange tongues (and forget English), remain insensate for days. At first some of them reported communications from "our Heavenly Parents"—Jesus and Mother Ann. Soon came visions of the early elders, and then of departed Shakers, followed by heavenly entities—the Sounding Angel, the Angel of Love, the Angel Gabriel, the Angel of Consuming Fire, the Holy Witnessing Angel. Messages also came from the prophets and the Apostles, and then from the Persian ruler Xerxes, from Alexander the Great, Queen Elizabeth I, Napoleon, George Washington, and Lafayette, William Penn, and other lesser historical figures. The visions and revelations had a purpose: Through them Mother Ann asked for a return to earlier principles, stressing simplicity in attire and furnishings, and the need for honest labor.

In 1841, Holy Mother Wisdom began to appear to the women and then to entire communities. The faithful would prepare themselves in advance by praying, fasting on bread and water, and cleaning up the buildings. The mystical figure was not seen in person, but she spoke through certain people favored by her visions.

There were other changes, too. Healing by faith became popular, though the Society continued to rely on herbals and a few simple medicines. Pork was eventually forbidden, along with tobacco and strong drink. Many people became vegetarians, though abstinence from meat never became official.

Throughout the entire history of the Shakers the sexes were

always kept separate. But they could sing together and pass sociable evenings under controlled conditions. Some of the young people, brought to the communities as orphans, or passed over by parents too poor to raise them, refused to join as adults. Many paired off and left.

It was the doctrine of marriage versus celibacy, the doctrine that had been so crucial to Mother Ann, Meacham, and the elders, that finally brought an end to the Shakers. Without children born into the communities, and having to rely upon converts or the adoption of young children who would remain Shakers, the society began to decline. The Shakers were also subject to attacks by missionaries from other churches. Joseph Smith saw the Shakers as likely converts to Mormonism, and he sent missionaries to North Union. There was a violent argument over marriage—"lust" as the Believers saw it, necessarily polygamous in the eyes of the Mormons, who interpreted Scripture differently—and over the nature of "messiahship"—Mother Ann as the Second Coming, versus Joseph Smith as the messenger of God. The debate became bitter, and the Mormons were expelled instead of being given the honors normally accorded visitors.

After the Civil War the Shakers entered a notable decline. The entire continent was opening up to the young and adventurous, and a quiet life in a remote community, however well run, had less and less appeal to the nation. By the end of the nineteenth century, entire communities (there had been nineteen major centers and ten missions and "out families" at the height of the movement) were closed irrevocably. The empty buildings were pulled down by the survivors, who were then absorbed into other villages, until they, too, died out. Today a few remaining Shaker villages have become historical landmarks and tourist attractions. Shaker furniture commands premium prices and is much copied. The Trappist writer and monk, Thomas Merton, who made a study of the Shaker community at Pleasant Hill, Kentucky, observed that too late we have "recognized the extraordinary importance of the spiritual phenomenon that had blossomed out in their midst . . . their unique combination of 'science, religion and inspiration,' which remains to us a mysterious and fascinating 'sign' for our times."

3

☆   ☆   ☆   ☆   ☆   ☆   ☆   ☆   ☆

THE MORMONS

ONE BEAUTIFUL, CLEAR SPRING DAY IN 1820, JOSEPH Smith, Jr., third son of a poor farmer in Palmyra, New York, had a vision. Smith was only a few months past his fourteenth birthday. He was a rather serious young man, given to speculation about worldly events, and even more so, religion. Upstate New York, which was then sparsely settled by New Englanders (the Smiths had come from Vermont, where Smith was born), still had enough inhabitants to be the scene of religious controversies between the various Protestant sects, especially the Methodists, Presbyterians, and Baptists. Communities and even families were split by intense battles. Churches, houses, and barns were set on fire by all sides so that, as mentioned earlier, this area of the state was known as "the burned-over district." The teen-age Smith was so disturbed by the arguments that swirled about him that they occupied his thoughts in a morbid manner. "In the midst of this war of words and tumult of opinions," he wrote later, "I often said to myself, what is to be done? Who of all these parties be right? Or are they all wrong together?"

Even his own family was not spared from the controversies. Smith's mother, two of his brothers, and his sister, Sophronia, joined the Presbyterians. But, Smith wrote, "In the process of time my mind became somewhat partial to the Methodist sect." His feelings during this period were "deep and pungent," but he still felt uneasy over his selection of a church. One day while reading the Epistle of Saint James, he was struck by the applicability of the fifth verse of the first chapter.

If any of you lack wisdom, let him ask of God, that giveth unto all men liberally and unbraideth not; and it shall be given him.

With this he decided that either he must remain in darkness and confusion, or follow James's advice. Shortly afterward he went out into the woods, knelt down, and began to pray. The result was astonishing.

Immediately I was seized upon by some power which entirely overcame me, and had such astounding influence over me as to bind my tongue so that I could not speak.

Thick darkness engulfed the boy, and he felt lost.

Just at this moment of great alarm, I saw a pillar of light exactly over my head, above the brightness of the sun; which descended gradually until it fell upon me. . . . When the light rested upon me I saw two personages (whose brightness and glory defy all description) standing above me in the air.

The two personages were God the Father and Jesus, the former saying to Smith, "This is My beloved Son, hear Him." Smith asked Jesus which church he should join. Jesus answered, "None of them, for they were all wrong," and that all their creeds were an abomination in His sight.

When Smith came to his senses he found himself lying on his back looking up into heaven. A few days after the vision Smith tried to tell one of the local ministers about his experience but was informed that the day of visions and revelations had passed, and from then on he was the object of persecution from all the ministers of the various churches. "However, it was nevertheless a fact that I had had a vision."

Young Smith continued as a farm laborer. Only the members of his family accepted the fact of his vision; the rest of the community continued to persecute Smith.

Forbidden by Jesus to join any of the established churches, young Smith "frequently fell into many foolish errors, and displayed the weakness of youth and the foibles of human nature. On the night of September 21, 1823, while he was praying to God for the forgiveness of his sins (not any "great or malignant sins," Smith admits), he had a second divine vision.

A light appeared in the room which continued to increase until the room was lighter than at noonday, when immediately a personage appeared at my bedside standing in the air, for his feet did not touch the floor. [Smith describes the apparition in detail, and then says] He called me by name, and said unto me that he was a messenger sent from the presence of God to me, and that his name was Moroni. That God had work for me to do, and that my name should be had for good and evil, among all nations, kindreds, and tongues. . . .

He said that there was a book deposited written upon gold plates, giving an account of the former inhabitants of this continent, and the source from whence they sprang.

The angel Moroni quoted various scriptural passages to Smith, some of them at variance with the accepted text of the King James version, which was then commonly used by all the churches except the Roman Catholic. The angel eventually disappeared into heaven, leaving the room in darkness. But he soon returned in a flood of light, to repeat without variation what he had told Smith earlier. Then . . .

. . . he informed me of great judgments which were coming upon the earth, with great desolations by famine, sword and pestilence, and that these grievous judgments would come on the earth in this generation.

Moroni appeared a third time, repeating what he had said earlier, and warning Smith that he would be tempted to sell the golden plates because of his family's poverty.

The next day Smith collapsed while working alongside his father, and he started to go home. On the way, an angel appeared and told him to return to the fields, and to inform his father of the earlier visions. The elder Smith told his son to do as the angel had instructed. Young Joseph then sought out the hill—which the Mormons call Mount Cumorah—where the angel had informed him the gold tablets were buried. He found them under a stone of considerable size in a stone box. In the box were the golden plates, along with "Urim and Thummim," the Breastplate of the High Priest of the Temple in Jerusalem. Smith made an attempt to remove the objects from the box, but was told by the angel that he must wait four years, though he was to visit the site every year on the same date.

Smith began to work for another farmer in the area, then was persuaded by an elderly eccentric to go to Harmony, Pennsylvania, to look for some rumored Spanish gold mines. In Harmony, Smith met Emma Hale, who was to become his wife. Emma's family was opposed to Smith, so he brought her back to New York, where the young couple was married in January 1827, four weeks after Smith's twenty-first birthday.

This same year—1827—was the one in which Smith had been given permission by Moroni to remove the golden plates from their burial chamber on Mount Cumorah. Once more Moroni instructed him not to let the plates out of his hands; there would be many attempts to take them, warned the angel. What actually happened at this point is not clear from the Mormon records. Why Smith informed anyone else is a mystery, but "strenuous exertions were made by wicked persons to get it [the plates] out of his hands. . . . Conjurors, diviners with peepstones and other means were employed." Mobs searched the Smith home and ransacked it. Smith hid the plates in odd places—a hollow log and a barrel of beans were among them.

Meanwhile Smith prepared to translate the text of the plates. His wife's family, the Hales, had reconciled themselves to the marriage, and invited him to Harmony. Smith bought a small farm where he could work in peace on the tablets. He made a copy of the characters on the plates, which "consisted of the learning of the Jews and the language, in hieroglyphics, of the Egyptians." With the aid of Urim and Thummim, Smith made a partial translation. What Urim and Thummim were is not entirely clear, at least to the outsider. In ancient Jerusalem they were objects attached to the Breastplate of the High Priest and were used by him to ascertain the will of God on questions of national importance to the Israelites after their return from Babylonian captivity. In the case of Smith's tablets from Mount Cumorah, they seemed to have been the means of turning the ancient characters into modern English.

What Joseph Smith actually transcribed from the tablets shown him by the angel Moroni is a mystery today. These lines are purported to be fair copies of "Caractors" written down by Smith.

A friend, Marvin Harris, saw the beginning of Smith's translation and asked if he could take it, along with the copy of the tablets, to New York. What happened next was something of a tragedy. Harris showed the work to a Professor Charles Anthon of Columbia College. According to Harris, Anthon said that the translation was correct, more so than any he had seen before translated from the Egyptian. He told Harris that the rest of the characters were Egyptian, Chaldaic, Assyrian, and Arabic, and he gave Harris a certificate testifying to that fact, and also to the correctness of the translation.

After Harris had put the certificate in his pocket, Anthon asked him how Smith had gotten possession of the gold plates. Harris replied that "an angel of God had revealed it unto him." Whereupon, Harris said, Anthon took the certificate from him, tore it up, and said there was no longer any such thing as the ministering of angels. Anthon wanted to see the original tablets, but Harris replied that he was forbidden to bring them to anyone else. Years later Anthon admitted that a man named Harris had come to see him, but he had thought the entire thing was a hoax.

Smith continued to translate the tablets, with Harris taking down what he dictated. By early April 1828, Smith had translated enough text to fill 128 handwritten pages. At this point Harris wanted to take the text home to show to skeptical friends who had criticized him for wasting his time. Smith inquired of Urim and Thummim if Harris might have the pages and he was denied. A second request was also denied, but the third was accepted with limited conditions about who was to see the translation. Needless to say, in his enthusiasm Harris showed too many people the translation, and "by strategem it passed out of his hands."

For days Smith was in anguish over the loss and his part in it. Eventually Moroni appeared, first to rebuke Smith, but then to say he would be given permission to continue with his work. The gold plates and the Urim and Thummim were temporarily taken from him, then returned. The missing pages were not to be retranslated. Harris was never permitted again to work as a scribe, and his place was taken by a young teacher named Oliver Cowdery, from New York State. Cowdery had been given a revelation about Smith, and he went to Harmony to investigate, with the result that he joined wholeheartedly into the translation.

About five weeks after Cowdery's arrival, both he and Smith underwent a visionary experience. During the translating, both men noticed that the tablets gave a different interpretation on the question of baptism for the remission of sins from what the established churches taught. They went into the woods to pray to God for enlightenment. A "heavenly messenger descended in a cloud of light and said he was John the Baptist," acting "under the direction of Peter, James and John, who held the keys of the Melchezidek Priesthood, and had been sent to confer on Joseph and Oliver the Aaronic Priesthood, which holds the keys to the temporal Gospel."

John laid his hands upon their heads, and in the name of Jesus the Messiah gave them the power of ministering of the angels and of the Gospel, and of baptism by immersion. The Melchezidek Priesthood would also be conferred, soon, said John, and Joseph Smith would be called the first and Oliver Cowdery the second elder of the Church. John then instructed both to go to the water and baptize each other.

Meanwhile Smith's father-in-law, Isaac Hale, began to oppose the work of translation. Smith and Cowdery moved to Fayette, located between lakes Cayuga and Seneca in upper New York State. Here they were taken in by David Whitmer, who was very much interested in what Smith and Cowdery had been experiencing. Soon they made several converts, baptizing Smith's younger brother, Samuel, and then some others. The translation of *The Book of Mormon* was completed in June 1829. The group gathered around Joseph Smith had, more or less, spontaneously formed itself into the nucleus of a church. Every morning they gathered at the Whitmer home to pray and to sing.

Meanwhile it occurred to Cowdery, Whitmer, and Harris that they might be privileged to see the golden plates. With Smith they retired to the woods to pray, but received no answer giving permission for others to view the tablets. After a second request failed, Harris voluntarily withdrew on the grounds that his earlier behavior had angered the Lord. This time an angel appeared with the plates in the usual aura of light, holding them and turning each leaf one by one. Above the angel a voice said:

These plates have been revealed by the power of God, and they have been translated by the power of God; the translation of them which you have seen is correct, and I command you to bear record of what you now see and hear.

Smith called out to Harris, who had not gone far away, and he, too, was privileged to see the plates in the hands of the angel. All three men attested to what they had witnessed and heard, and stated, "We know of a surety that the work is true."

These were not the only witnesses to the plates. Smith himself was empowered to show them to his father and two brothers, to four members of the Whitmer family, and to a man named Hiram Page. But controversy eventually surrounded the testimony of these witnesses. Both Cowdery and Harris were later estranged from Smith and excommunicated from the Church, only to be readmitted years afterward. David Whitmer, also estranged, never returned. But before his death, he refuted reports that he had called the tablets false. Not long after he had been a witness to the tablets, Hiram Page experienced a revelation with a "stone" which the others said was not true. In 1838, Page left the Church never to return.

Whatever the problems, Smith was able to get the manuscript of *The Book of Mormon* to a printer in Palmyra. Five thousand copies were printed at the then considerable cost of three thousand dollars, and distribution of the work began to the faithful and the potentially faithful.

The Book of Mormon is one of those curious documents which are either totally inspiring or totally baffling. It is easy to criticize the circumstances in which it was produced—an uneducated young farmhand finding plates of gold under the direction of an angel, and translating them into idiomatic nineteenth-century upper New York State English with the aid of two strange implements, Urim and Thummim, from ancient and complicated Middle Eastern languages. Whether the Mormon version of the circumstances is true, or there is another explanation, we cannot know today. But *The Book of Mormon* exists, mysteriously, inexplicably.

The Mormons do not consider The Book another "Bible," nor a substitute for the original Scriptures, but a complementary work, with a special revelation for the New World, just as the Old and New Testaments were revelations for the ancient world.

The work tells of a tribe, the Jaredites, members of the House of Israel and ancestors of the American Indian, who along with others, among them the perpetually warring Nephites and Lamanites, came to this continent in the seventh century before Christ (the chronology covers the period roughly from 600 B.C. to A.D. 421). During the reign of King Zedekiah they left Jerusalem, and eventually crossed the oceans to the west, where they built great cities and civilizations. But in their wars with each other they destroyed themselves.

The tribes had brought with them certain records of the Old Testament, along with records of important events in their own civilization preserved by their prophets, historians, and rulers. Some of this material was engraved on the gold plates revealed to Smith. The book takes its title from the prophet Mormon, the last great leader of the Nephites. Mormon had resigned as leader because of the wickedness of his people; he assembled the various records and hid them in Mount Cumorah, and was killed in a battle with the Lamanites.

As descendants of one of the tribes of Israel, the American Indians have been a special goal of Mormon proselytizing, but with no great success. The Mormons believe that the Indians are the descendants of Ephraim and Manessah, the sons of Joseph. America is theirs by God-given right, and is referred to in the Old Testament by Jacob, Moses, Ezekiel, and Isaiah, as the land of the restored Israel, where the "Little Stones of Israel" will smote the pagan image in Daniel 2: 34–35 (a most obscure reference to the uninitiated).

THE CHURCH OF JESUS CHRIST OF LATTER-DAY SAINTS

With *The Book of Mormon* safely translated and in type, Smith next took the steps of organizing his small flock. In April 1830, in a meeting at the Whitmers', he asked if the group should not be formally established as a church. The consensus was yes, and Smith laid hands upon Oliver Cowdery and ordained him an elder of the "Church of Jesus Christ of Latter-day Saints" (they had begun to call themselves "Saints"). Cowdery next ordained Smith. A communion service was held, with bread, which was blessed with the new powers of the two elders, and wine, also blessed. Everyone present participated in the sacred foods.

Others were ordained after that, and Smith could write in his short testament to his brief ministry of the "pleasing knowledge" that the Mormons had organized in accordance with the commandments and revelations given them by God "in the last day." He and the others were convinced that Jesus would soon return (the date was not established precisely as in other sects), and that this was in truth the final preparation, the true Restoration of the time for Christ's fulfillment of His mission to mankind.

New members came in regularly to the young church. Shortly after the first ordination, Smith performed his first miracle and cast out an evil spirit from a young man, named Newel Knight, who had all the signs of demonic possession. Converts by the dozens were baptized by Smith and the other elders. However, much resentment developed among members of the older churches. There was at least one case of what is now called "deprogramming"—an effort by a Presbyterian minister to abduct a young woman sympathetic to the Mormons and to prevent her conversion. Nevertheless, she was baptized.

Finally, after many threats of violence by mobs, a warrant was obtained against Smith and he was arrested on the charge of being a "disorderly person." The charges were dismissed in court. A second warrant in another town brought Smith to court again, and the charges in this case, too, were dismissed. However, mobs continued to harass the Mormons as they preached.

Meanwhile, revelations continued unabated. In the summer of 1830 Smith "received the words of the Lord to Moses" at a time when Moses had ascended a mountain to talk to God face to face. Other writings of Moses were later revealed to Smith, among them the document known as the Pearl of Great Price. In July of

Mormon elders at the communion table, the Lord's Supper being observed each Sunday. The Mormons believe in Christ's return to earth, in the gift of tongues, visions, continuing prophecy, and healing, and that God the Father and Jesus Christ have bodies of flesh and bones as tangible as man's, but that the Holy Ghost is a spirit.

the same year, 1830, Smith and Oliver Cowdery had a vision of the Lord, in which He counseled them to be patient in the many afflictions they were about to experience. In the same month Emma Smith, the Prophet's wife, was told by the Lord not to talk about things—revelations—she had not seen. At the same time He informed her that she had been chosen to make a selection of sacred hymns for the church. It was a time of continuing revelations, and others of the elders were honored. However, some of the faithful claimed, falsely, that they, too, had experienced visions and revelations. This was a problem that was to plague the church in the coming years—which revelations were true and which were not.

The first major group of missionaries were four young converts who went to Ohio to preach to members of a new sect known as both the Campbellites and the Disciples. It was a fundamentalist group and saw the Bible as the only means to salvation. One of the Campbellites was Sidney Rigdon, who was to play an important role in Mormon history. The Campbellites were centered in Kirtland, Ohio, and here Rigdon and his wife were baptized as Mormons and led a large number of Campbellites into the new church. Now a revelation commanded Smith to gather the scattered groups of Saints together and to lead them into Ohio in order to get away from the continual persecution of the Mormons by enemies. In February 1831, the church was formally established in Kirtland, along somewhat communal lines of property and duty. The revelation at that time promised a "new Jerusalem, or city of Zion," the site to be announced later.

Others also had been receiving revelations, but in March Smith received one which instructed the church that only his revelations were authentic. In March, also, the Second Coming of Jesus was announced.

The Lord made known many things . . . pertaining to his second coming and the signs of the times. . . . He spoke of the signs and wonders; of the gathering of the Jews [after their exile]; the darkening of the sun and the bathing of the moon in blood; of his second coming and his judgments upon nations; the redemption of the Jews, who shall look upon him whom they have pierced; the binding of satan; the millennial reign; and the redemption of heathen nations and those who knew no law.

It was a period of millennial expectations among many Christians, and William Miller, a farmer in New York State, had already announced that the world would end in 1843 (see "The Millennium: Adventists and Witnesses," page 92). What influence Miller's teachings had upon the Mormons is difficult to establish at this point. Members continued to arrive in Kirtland from New York, and missionaries kept pushing westward. The lands were filled with both Indian tribes and renegade whites—"devils from the infernal pit, united and foaming out their shame"—as well as "Universalists, Atheists, Presbyterians, Methodists, Baptists, and other professing Christians." The Mormons were now ordered by revelation to descend into the heart of this maelstrom to found the New Zion, in western Missouri. The site was a hamlet called Independence.

Said the Lord to Smith:

Behold, the place which is now called Independence, is the center place; and a spot for the temple is lying westward, upon a lot which is not far from the courthouse. Wherefore, it is wisdom that the land should be purchased by the saints, and also every tract lying westward, even unto the line running directly between Jew and Gentile. . . .

Land was bought as the Lord had directed, a little west of the Independence courthouse. In August 1831, the site was dedicated for a great temple to be built later. New members arrived regularly from New York, among them Brigham Young, who was to become one of the church's greatest leaders. Revelations about Mormon doctrine, policy, and works continued unabated. But harassment from "enemies" also continued. While the colony was establishing itself in Missouri in its new Zion, mobs continued to attack the faithful. In April 1833, a crowd of three hundred met to try to force the Mormons from Missouri; nothing came of the attempt, but anti-Mormon resentment grew.

Smith ordered work to begin on the temple, but before anything substantial could be accomplished, the Mormons were driven from Independence. However, they were able to build and dedicate another temple in Kirtland. Then internal difficulties plagued the Mormons. Not only were false visions and revelations rampant, but some of the faithful either apostacized or were excommunicated. Also, there was at least one attempt to depose Smith and replace him with David Whitmer. In this instance the Kirtland group was responsible, with the result that the new temple was lost to Smith's party. Brigham Young, Smith, and Sidney Rigdon, who were in Kirtland at the time of the quarrel, fled to Missouri. Despite the battles, a mission to England was founded, with considerable success.

In Missouri, events moved from one crisis to another. Armed clashes between Mormons, mobs, local police, and state militia became frequent. Governor Lilburn W. Boggs ordered the militia to be held ready for major action against the Mormons, who, he believed, were conspiring with the Indians to rise against the state. A major battle at Crooked River resulted in the death of several Mormons. By October 1838, Boggs received highly exaggerated reports that the Mormons were looting and burning, and he ordered their "extermination."

The Mormons must be treated as enemies and must be exterminated or driven from the state, if necessary, for the public good. Their outrages are beyond all description.

By this time there were twelve thousand Mormons in Missouri. The militia began to shoot them down in their communities as ruthlessly as federal troops then and later shot down Indians. It was a major war; the Mormons, who were well armed, began to fight back, but eventually Smith and other leaders were captured. A court martial was held, and the prisoners were ordered to be shot by a firing squad. There was dissension among the militia officers about the legality of executing them. The brigadier general given the assignment refused to carry it out and the executions never took place. But the state of war continued, with arrests, murders, mob violence, and trials which usually resulted in the Mormons being found not guilty. Many of the faithful were driven from Missouri and went westward.

While the troubles continued in Missouri, Smith sought out other sites in the Midwest where his people could live in safety and without harassment. Moving up the Mississippi to where it forms a border between Iowa and Illinois, he found a small hamlet called Commerce, on the eastern shore of the river, where it made a loop so that the town was bound on three sides by water, and overlooked rolling fertile plains to the east. Much of the land was swampy, but Smith saw that it could be drained. Taking possession of the site in the spring of 1839, Smith changed the name to Nauvoo, which he said meant "a beautiful place" in Hebrew. Other lands were bought for Mormon settlements in Illinois and across the river in Iowa.

Nauvoo became a center for the Saints' activities, and a holy city was built in seven years out of what had been marshland and half a dozen or so log cabins and rough wood-frame houses. It soon had 2,200 houses, 300 of them brick (much of the architecture was patterned after the old Dutch houses of New York State), twenty schools, a university, five potteries and four bakeries, three newspapers, and whatever else a small city required. In fact, at the time Nauvoo was equal to Chicago in size, and because of the hard work, intelligence, dedication, and relative sophistication of its inhabitants (mostly easterners and English immigrant converts) it was far advanced in comparision to other prairie towns.

The central feature of Nauvoo was the huge temple set on a hill dominating the town and the landscape. Made of limestone after an eclectic design received by Smith in visions, it was 88 feet wide by 128 feet in length, with a tower 158½ feet high topped with a gilded statue of the angel Moroni.

The next five years were no better for the Mormons, despite their new settlements in areas where they hoped to experience less prejudice and hostility. The situation was not eased when Smith let it be known that he had received a revelation allowing "plural marriage," to others nothing but polygamy. The doctrine was not officially announced until 1852, in Salt Lake City, and it was stressed by the elders that it was not meant to "gratify the carnal lusts and feelings of men," but to be practiced in all holiness.

The final crisis came in June 1844, when Smith was charged with several offenses, chief of which was an effort to close down a newspaper just begun by a dissident group of Mormons in Nauvoo. An attempt had already been made on Smith's life, and mobs in Missouri, Iowa, and Illinois had pledged their common allegiance to drive out the Saints. Everyday violence was now a matter of course. Smith appealed to the governor for protection; the governor, Thomas Ford, in turn ordered Smith's arrest. Smith and some others, including his brother Hyrum, decided to flee to the Rockies, but his wife Emma sent a letter after him accusing him of cowardice. Smith returned to Nauvoo, was arrested with his brother Hyrum, and was taken by the posse to Carthage, the state capital.

I am going like a lamb to the slaughter [said Smith]. *But I am as calm as a summer's morning. I have a conscience void of offense toward God and toward all men. If they take my life I shall die an innocent man, and my blood shall cry from the ground for ven-*

geance, and it shall be said of me, "He was murdered in cold blood."

Joseph and Hyrum, along with some other Saints, were imprisoned in Carthage on the basis of some legal documents the Mormons claimed were forged. They spent most of the night discussing the Scriptures with other members of the church, and much of the following day, June 27, in prayer. Shortly after five in the afternoon, about one hundred armed men stormed the jail. The Smith brothers and Elder John Taylor had obtained guns from their visitors, but their pitiful arms were of no use. In the brief battle that followed, Hyrum Smith was shot down. Though wounded, Joseph Smith tried to escape through a window, but was shot again fatally as he leaped. Elder Taylor was seriously wounded. The mob suddenly withdrew as it saw the awful results of its strange anger. Taylor, an Englishman, lived to be able to go to England and France as a missionary, and later he became third president of the church.

The bodies of the martyrs were brought to Nauvoo for burial. Here, as elsewhere, the Mormons, understandably infuriated, and heavily armed, refused, however, to strike back at their oppressors and persecutors.

Now another crisis struck the Saints: Who was to succeed Smith? The battle that followed was as devastating as any with mobs and militia, for it was Mormon against Mormon.

THE MORMON CHURCHES

When the two Smiths were murdered, most of the Mormon leaders were away on missions. The struggle for control centered on two men, Brigham Young and Sidney Rigdon. Young was in Missouri at the time of the martyrdom, Rigdon in Pennsylvania. A group of the elders came together in August to decide upon the next leader. Rigdon claimed that there could be no single successor to Smith, but that there should be a "guardian" of the church. He stated he had received a vision to that effect. Rigdon spoke to a crowd of the faithful assembled in a grove in Nauvoo for an hour and a half, but the people drifted away. In the afternoon Young also addressed the crowd, with astonishing results.

When he first arose to speak the people were greatly astonished, for President Young stood transfixed before them, and they beheld the Prophet Joseph Smith and heard his voice as naturally as they ever did when he was living. It was a manifestation to the Saints that they might recognize the correct authority.

What happened then is a matter Mormons are still disputing. Rigdon refused to submit to Young and was excommunicated. At that point Brigham Young was president of the Quorum of the Twelve Apostles but not president of the church. He had the votes of eight of the twelve elders; the others were absent. On that basis, he took control, an act that other claimants said was illegal. Various dissidents refused to recognize Young's authority and several schisms came about.

Conditions in Nauvoo and elsewhere continued to deteriorate. Young decided that the Saints had to find a refuge so far away that there would be no harassment from unbelievers. His goal was the Rocky Mountains. In February 1846, the Mormons began to abandon all their settlements and head west. On the trek, one of unexpected severity and hardship, Young was confirmed as president of the church. His opponents then, and dissident Mormons today, claim that the election was not valid because there were only four members of the Quorum voting. This challenge has been ignored by the largest body of the Saints, those who finally found a sanctuary in the valley of Salt Lake and established the organization most people assume to be the only Mormon church in America.

Most of the church had left Nauvoo early. A remnant remained behind, finishing the temple and dedicating it on May 1, 1846, a few months after the westward trek had begun. The next day it was stripped down to bare walls, and all removable objects were loaded into wagons. The last of the Nauvoo Saints followed the others to Salt Lake. Two years later the temple was burned to the ground by an arsonist.

Rigdon was not the only man to claim the right of succession to Joseph Smith. Shortly before the martyrdom, James J. Strang had joined the Mormons at Nauvoo. Strang produced a letter he said had been written by the Prophet appointing him as successor. Strang gathered a substantial following and established himself on Beaver Island in Lake Michigan, where he was crowned king in 1850. Strang's rule was short-lived. One of his followers shot him six years later, and the Strangites (as they were known) fell to pieces. Like other Mormon leaders, Strang experienced visions, and in common with some of them, he found "ancient" texts, which he translated for the faithful. One of his major achievements is a work called *The Book of the Law of the Lord*, and another *The Voree Record*. The latter text was found under an oak tree near Voree, Wisconsin, and was in hieroglyphic characters composed by "an ancient people . . . who no longer exist." The church, which calls itself the Church of the Latter-Day Saints, Strangites, admits to a "lack of prophetic leadership at the present time." There are about three hundred members in six churches.

Many of the early Strangites went to still another organization, the Reorganized Church of Jesus Christ of Latter-Day Saints. The Reorganized Church was built from a collection of forces opposed to the rule of Brigham Young, a man enemies described as "possessed with a cruel and remorseless ambition." Their first meeting was held in 1852 in Beloit, Wisconsin, and they were formally organized in 1860 at Amboy, Illinois. The Reorganized Church made the obvious and wise decision to choose the martyred Prophet's son Joseph Smith, III, as president. All the presidents of this church have been descendants of the founder, thus giving it a legitimacy that the others cannot easily claim. Next to the Utah organization of Mormons, it is the largest and most successful group, with nearly a quarter of a million members.

Of the other splinter groups ("splinter" is perhaps an unfair term, for each church of Mormons believes itself the true church and regards the others as heretics), the most important is the Church of Christ. It is identified with the words "Temple Lot," for it possesses several temple lots in Independence, Missouri. These are the original portions dedicated by Joseph Smith in 1831 for the building of the Lord's Temple. Since the original building was interrupted by the turmoil surrounding the Mormons in Missouri, the Church of Christ believes that the Lord Himself will designate the time of building. While the members of the church cannot begin work until the "appointed time," it is still their sacred responsibility to hold the land and keep it free so "that when the time of building does come, it can be accomplished as the Lord sees fit."

The temple lots were the center of much controversy between the Church of Christ (not to be confused with non-Mormon churches with the same name) and the Reorganized Church of Jesus Christ of Latter-Day Saints. The Reorganized Church lost the battles, but the victor has not profited to any great extent so far as worldly and supernatural successes can be measured. Today the Church of Christ has only about three thousand members in some thirty-two local congregations.

Such was the founding of the "Mormon" church, so-called because it was based upon *The Book of Mormon.* But as Smith stated in the ordination ceremony, it was properly the "Church of Jesus Christ of Latter-day Saints."

The church, according to Mormons, is not a new church, nor is it a Protestant church. Certainly it is not the Roman Catholic Church, nor a branch of it. To Mormons it is nothing less than the original church of Jesus, the apostles, and disciples, restored to its original truth, beauty, and sanctity. But the restored church has more, for it preaches that revelation continues, and does not end with the apostolic period. Doctrines made known to Joseph Smith and his successors are in fulfillment of God's promises to Adam.

Doctrines revealed to, or at least taught by, the Mormons are at variance with those of other Christian churches. To begin with, the Mormons believe the Gospel "existed before the foundation of the world." They believe Adam was sent to earth as the progenitor of the human race—the Mormons do not accept Darwinian evolution—and was baptized with water for the remission of his sins. But by the time of Noah all but a few of mankind had rejected God's teachings. Abraham preached the Gospel, but the children of

Israel rejected it. Thus the law of Moses was given as preparation for the coming of Jesus, who restored the Gospel and ordained twelve apostles, who were commanded to teach throughout the world.

The Mormons explain that for a while the church was "perfect," but that then a "strange organization" appeared which perverted the teachings of God. That organization was the Church of Rome, which introduced such customs as baptism by the sprinkling of water in place of total immersion, a celibate clergy, changes in the administration of the Lord's Supper, and so on. The cruel institution known as the Inquisition persecuted those who refused to submit to the power of Rome, and the sale of indulgences in the Middle Ages was a blasphemous doctrine of forgiving sins. The Protestant Reformation ended many of the abuses of Rome, but marvelous, reasonable, and scriptural as it was, the Reformation was only what its name said, not a restoration of the true church. This Mormons believe was why Joseph Smith was called.

The various Mormon churches are united in many things. A chief belief is the infallibility of the Bible and the prophetic calling of Joseph Smith to restore the ancient church founded by Jesus and propagated by the disciples and early elders. Each church has the firm conviction that it alone is the true church and that the others are in error, as are the Roman Catholics and the various Protestant denominations and their successors. All Mormons share such common doctrines as a belief in the necessity of certain types of officers in the ancient church—apostles, evangelists, elders, teachers, deacons, and so on—the laying on of hands, the resurrection of the dead, a final and eternal judgment, the use of the term "Saints" for the true followers of Jesus, continuing revelations in the present day, and other teachings. They differ widely, however, in many ways. The Monongahela Mormons, descended from Sidney Rigdon's church, believe that baptism must be bestowed upon adults only by immersion in natural bodies of water. Other Mormons allow baptism for children age eight and up, both in the open and in pools. The Utah Mormons believe that baptism can be given to the dead, a doctrine the other churches view with horror.

The Reorganized Church believes that Smith's translation

of the Bible was inspired, the others do not. *The Book of Mormon* is treated differently in the various churches. The main group, that in Utah, now tends to play down the work, for its doctrines are often hard for more sophisticated members to accept. Utah literature often ignores The Book entirely, while other Mormon churches draw upon it as needed.

The various churches are supported by tithing—the gift of 10 percent of one's income to the church—and very few church executives are paid. In the Salt Lake City church each male is expected to serve a term as a missionary, without pay. Boys may often begin to practice on neighbors, and sooner or later, when they are in their teens or are of college age, they will go into non-Mormon areas and overseas. Mormon life is quite family- and church-centered, abstemious, hard-working, and charitable. Mormons do not drink or smoke, and medical surveys show that their death rate is "lower than that of any group of people the same size anywhere in the world."

The very controversial teaching of polygamy, which was for many years practiced by the Utah church, was denounced by the others. Eventually Salt Lake City was forced to abandon the teaching after the United States government made it clear that polygamy was against the law. Still, there is a remnant of Mormons, living quietly and otherwise subscribing to most of the teachings of the Utah church, who practice plural marriages. There are reported to be polygamous Mormons living in isolated areas of New Mexico and Arizona. All in all, whatever the differences in beliefs, most Mormons have shown themselves fervent in their faith, active proselytizers (Mormon missions abroad have been extremely successful), and convinced that theirs is the true restored church that Christ Himself founded.

4

CHRISTIAN SCIENCE

O N A COLD NEW ENGLAND DAY, THE FIRST OF FEBRU-
ary 1866, a slim, small-boned, dark-haired, attractive
woman named Mary Baker Patterson had an accident. It
was typical of the kind of accident that might strike anyone in
blustery, freezing weather. She slipped on the ice and badly hurt
herself.

The Lynn, Massachusetts, *Reporter* of Saturday, February
3, ran a brief paragraph about the incident.

Mrs. Mary Patterson of Swampscott fell upon the ice near the cor-
ner of Market and Oxford streets on Thursday evening and was se-
verely injured. She was taken up in an insensible condition and car-
ried into the residence of S. M. Bubier, Esq., near by, where she

was kindly cared for during the night. Dr. Cushing, who was called for, found her injuries to be internal and of a severe nature, inducing spasms and internal suffering. She was removed to her home in Swampscott yesterday afternoon, though in a very critical condition.

It was a more than an ordinary fall, and people despaired that Mrs. Patterson would not live. On the Sunday immediately after the accident, in her own home, a curious event took place. Asking her friends and a local Protestant minister to leave the bedroom where they had crowded around her in the very real expectation that she was dying, Mrs. Patterson said she wanted to be alone with her Bible. She turned to the passage in Matthew—second verse, ninth chapter—which tells of Jesus' healing of a palsied man. The result of her meditation upon this simple verse and her prayer to God was a moment that changed Mrs. Patterson's life forever and had a profound effect upon millions of people who later came under her guidance. She reported later that she had a flash of divine revelation. In that mystical and sacred instance which filled her receptive and eager consciousness, the grip of the disease that bound her to her bed was broken and she was immediately healed.

Mrs. Patterson arose from her bed, dressed, and walked into the parlor where the clergyman and her friends were waiting in an unhappy vigil for her death in the next room. Confusion and consternation reigned. There was doubt of a cure, but Mrs. Patterson was on her feet, walking and well again. The fact was that she had been divinely healed, she told her friends.

The cure had come with the speed of lightning, but the preparation for that wonderful moment had been a background of nearly forty years of intense study of the Bible. During that time Mrs. Patterson had worked out the rudimentary principles of divine healing which she was to effectively put into use to bring about her release from illness, and which later, as Mary Baker Eddy, gained her fame as the "Discoverer, Founder, and Leader" of Christian Science.

She was born Mary Morse Baker, in the very rural hamlet of Bow, New Hampshire, on July 16, 1821. She was the sixth and last child of Mark and Abigail Baker, each descended from a long line of upright and righteous church-going people, dating back to 1634. The parents were Congregationalists, members of the often stern and sometimes intolerant church that had been brought to New England by the Puritans and Pilgrims. One of Mary Baker Eddy's biographers reported that Mark Baker, a lawyer and gentleman farmer, believed in "a hard and bitter doctrine of pre-destination and . . . that a horrible decree of endless punishment awaited sinners on a final judgment day." Also, he accepted the doctrine of "unconditional election," that God chose only certain individuals for salvation.

Mary was a delicate child from birth. "Nervous ailments"— a catch-all phrase for nineteenth-century illnesses—and a spinal condition prevented her from regular attendance at school, though she was able to attend Sanbornton Academy and Holmes Academy later on. Beginning at the age of six she was tutored when necessary by her three older brothers, Samuel, Albert, and George, and two sisters, Abigail and Martha. Albert helped her learn English grammar and composition, and languages, among them Greek, Latin, and Hebrew. Her upbringing was conventional for New England at that time, except that Mary showed marked religious and altruistic tendencies. She enjoyed reading the Bible and could repeat sermons in detail.

By the age of twelve she was firmly committed to staying at home, sitting in her rocking chair, and reading the Bible rather than playing like other children. She was noted for her concern for people and for animals. On a few occasions she gave away her outer clothing—coat, hat, and mittens—to poor people during the winter. Friends recalled later that she took care of lonely children at school. She became a prolific poet and prose writer at school, and after graduation was a regular contributor to magazines and newspapers.

Her religious yearnings set her apart from other children. "From my very childhood I was impelled by a hunger and a thirst after divine things—" she wrote later "—a desire for something higher and better than matter, and apart from it,—to seek diligently for the knowledge of God as the one great and ever-present relief from human woes."

At the age of eight she had begun hearing voices, experiences that continued for a year. Often she would hear her name called out three times, each repetition on a higher tone. Mark Baker, a stern and rigorous man, given to long discussions and arguments with relatives and friends over religious subjects, was perplexed. Mystical experiences were outside his beliefs. "Take the book [the Bible] away from her," he said. "Her brain is too big for her body." Mary was sent out to play like other children. Her relationship with her father was tense. "Father kept the family in the tightest harness I have ever seen," she remarked later. His strict views on salvation as a mysterious reward for a chosen few by a punitive diety brought about a crisis with Mary when she was twelve, for she had frequently expressed her "confidence in God's love," a love that encompassed all. To her, everyone could be saved. The tensions remained, but at seventeen Mary joined the Congregational church of her parents, and apparently reached a compromise between the doctrine of God's selective grace and her own belief in universal salvation.

A romance. Brother Albert married. At the wedding Mary met a charming young ex-neighbor, Major George Washington Glover, a contractor and builder, who had been living in the South for the past four years. Timid Mary, so shy she would not enter the room where the wedding ceremony was being performed, struck the Major's eye.

The Major asked Mary to write to him in South Carolina, and in this way they became acquainted. "I became very fond of him," Mary recalled years afterward. Mark Baker was opposed to the budding romance, because he was afraid his daughter would be taken away from him. But shortly after, Mary's brother George said, "Mary, I have investigated and have found Major Glover a fine man. He has a good business and will make you a good husband."

Soon they were married—the year was 1843—and off the young couple went to Charleston, South Carolina. There was plenty

of southern charm, social life, lavish entertainment, and parties:
The scene was the romantic image of the old South. But it was a
society based on slavery. The new Mrs. Glover, who barely knew
her husband, was fiery with northern ideas about the abolition of
slavery, and she protested. Patiently, Major Glover explained that
not only was the economy of the South based upon slavery, but
that South Carolina had passed a law in 1820 forbidding the
freeing of slaves. To Mary Baker Glover the system was inherently
evil and wrong. She recalled later on:

*Even while in the South I did all I could to teach and preach abo-
lition, although it brought protests from my dear husband. . . . I
spoke freely against slavery and wrote vigorous articles in the press
in favor of freedom. This created such opposition that my husband
came to me and said that, although he had many friends, he did
not know that their friendship would save me, should it be known
that I was the advocate of freeing slaves.*

A short year after her marriage there came the first of many tragedies to strike Mary Baker. In June 1844, her husband died of yellow fever. Mary inherited his slaves, but abandoned her rights to
them, unable to give them their freedom under state law. "I de-
clined to sell them [the slaves] . . . for I could never believe that a
human being was my property." Mrs. Glover, six months pregnant,
returned to New Hampshire to live with her father. Her baby was
born and was named George. Distraught and frail after her husband's death, Mary Glover could not take care of the child, who
was given for the time to a nurse, Mahal Sanborn. Five years later,
Mark Baker's wife, Abigail, died, and the next year he remarried.
Mrs. Glover's stepmother did not want little George in the house;
in fact, Mary herself was not welcome, and so she moved into her
sister Abigail's house. Abigail, now married to a leading mill
owner, Alexander H. Tilton, also did not want George, and the boy
was again given into the care of Mahal Sanborn.

At Abigail's, the situation was difficult, for Abigail had no
use for Mary's intense religiosity and strange ideas. Mary was inclined to lie abed for long periods, afflicted with "spinal weak-

nesses" which caused "spasmodic seizures." The medical diagnosis was vague, but Mary Baker Glover was clearly unable to live a normal life. At times she had prostration and "complete nervous collapse." She often passed her day in a specially designed rocking chair in which she could be carried to her carriage and driven through the town and countryside.

A turning point in her life of tension and illness and estrangement from her son came when a dashing young man, Dr. Daniel Patterson, appeared on the scene. A dental surgeon of noted intellect and good reputation, Patterson could assure the anxious Mary that if they married, he would provide a home for young George. They did marry, but the doctor soon reneged on his promise. To see his mother, George was often forced to sneak in her window at night. Forlorn and unhappy with her life, Mrs. Patterson turned to the abolition movement. The nation was becoming more and more polarized over the issue of slavery. Mrs. Patterson wrote numerous articles on the subject for the New Hampshire *Patriot*, published in Concord. At times, when her health allowed, she worked as a substitute teacher at the New Hampshire Conference Seminary. But often she was forced to spend endless days in bed, weak and pale, an invalid. Her thoughts turned to the relationship between religion and health, between the mind and the body. For one long period she could eat nothing but bread, in another only grains and fruit. She eventually realized that semi-starvation was not acceptable to "wisdom" and as well was "equally far from Science, in which being is sustained by God, Mind."

Trying to find the key to the mysteries of life, of the universe, of God, she studied the medieval Christian philosophers, spiritualism and hypnotism, herbs and potions. She investigated hypnotism thoroughly (it was then often called mesmerism, after the Austrian physician F. A. Mesmer), so thoroughly that later she was accused of using it for healing others, a charge she was to reject. In 1860, young George, then sixteen, was forcibly taken away forever from Mrs. Patterson's care. What strange jealousies had been at work over Mary Patterson and her son are not clear, either from her own writings or the accounts of others. The references are ambiguous, and the root causes of the forced estrangement cannot be pinpointed. But her father, stepmother, sister, and her second husband all kept mother and son apart. Throughout her years, Mary Baker was much bothered by others who interfered in her life, close to the point of persecution, in order to "help" her. Such may have been the case with George. In her autobiographical *Retrospection and Introspection*, Mary wrote, "A plot was consummated for keeping us apart." George was given into the care of a family called the Chenrys, who took him to Minnesota. "Utter despair" was reported of his mother when that happened.

Even without this tragedy, life in the Patterson home was not easy. The doctor was casual, a spendthrift, and a sport. His practice was far less successful than he had promised, and as a sideline he took to running a sawmill. He was big, handsome, had great spirits, excessive self-confidence, and was a dandy: Even while hiking in the mountains the doctor would wear fine broadcloth and good linen, kid gloves and boots, a high hat. Life with sickly Mary Baker became too dull for this exuberant man, and he engaged in numerous affairs, often remaining away from home for days at a time. In 1861, the Civil War broke out, fanned partly by the question of states rights, partly by the question of slavery. The next year Dr. Patterson was sent by the governor of New Hampshire on a dangerous mission in the South, where he was to turn over funds to northern sympathizers. On his way home he was captured by Southern cavalry near Bull Run and imprisoned in one of the notorious Confederate stockades in the Deep South. He escaped, walked hundreds of miles to freedom, and found safety in Pennsylvania. It was an heroic adventure, but the doctor's character had not changed during his trials. He was still as impecunious and as unfaithful as ever.

QUIMBY AND MESMERISM

In perpetual ill health, spending days at a time on her bed of pain, the future blank, prayers unanswered, diets and health regimens useless, Mrs. Patterson looked for help from Phineas P. Quimby, a man whose name makes him sound like a typical nineteenth-century medicine man. Quimby was a "magnetic healer," and that designation put him in a shady light.

But he was an unusual man, and directly or indirectly he was to play an unusual role in nineteenth-century religious movements. Son of a poor blacksmith, apprenticed to a clockmaker, the builder of hundreds of clocks, tinkerer with small inventions, a tool maker who turned to the new art of the daguerrotype with some success, Quimby had found still another skill. Purely by chance he discovered that he was capable of putting people to sleep by hypnosis, or mesmerism, the preferred term at that time.

He was nervous, small, shrewd, argumentative, combative, inquiring, inventive, uneducated, and doggedly determined. He had piercing black eyes. "He refused to accept anything as a truth unless he could experiment with it himself and prove it for himself." He was not religious but "a man of good morals and of a kindly nature, always ready to help his neighbor."

After meeting the French hypnotist Charles Poyen in Belfast, Maine, in 1838, Quimby began to experiment with mesmerism. His efforts were not appreciated in Belfast, whose citizens greatly exaggerated Quimby's powers. More receptive fields were sought without success. Back in Belfast, after some wandering among suspicious New Englanders, he continued his work in mesmerism. By 1859 he had found a permanant home in Portland, where he gained many patients and was credited with numerous cures. Quimby was not above advertising his skills. He had written of himself (in the third person):

A gentleman of Belfast, Dr. Phineas P. Quimby, who was remarkably successful as an experimenter in mesmerism some sixteen years ago, and has continued his investigations in psychology, has discovered and in his daily practice carries out, a new principle in the treatment of disease.

His theory is that the mind gives immediate form to the animal spirit and that the animal spirit gives form to the body as soon as the less plastic elements of the body are able to assume that form. Therefore, the first course in the treatment of a patient is to sit down beside him and put himself in rapport with him, which he does without producing the mesmeric sleep.

He says that in every disease the animal spirit, or spiritual form, is somewhat disconnected from the body, that it imparts to *him all its grief and the cause of it, which may have been mental trouble or shock to the body, as over-fatigue, excessive cold or heat, etc. This impresses the mind with anxiety and the mind reacting upon the body produces disease. With this spirit form Dr. Quimby converses and endeavours to win it away from its grief, and when he has succeeded in doing so, it disappears and re-unites with the body. Thus is commenced the first step toward recovery. This union frequently lasts but a short time when the spirit again appears, exhibiting some new phase of its trouble. With this he again persuades and contends until he overcomes it, when it disappears as before. Thus two shades of trouble have disappeared from the mind and consequently from the animal spirit, and the body already has commenced its efforts to come into a state in accordance with them.*

By the 1860s Quimby had developed his thought to the point where he believed that man was a spiritual being, that the "wisdom" common to all men is Almighty God in man. Thus the soul was linked to the divine mind in an intimate relationship. The terms later popularized by Mary Baker, "Christian science" and "science of health," were part of Quimby's vocabulary. Moreover, Quimby stated that he was following the methods of Jesus.

Quimby's beliefs were a precursor of Christian Science, and he played a controversial role in the new religion. The Christian Scientists minimize his part in Mary Baker's life and his effect on her thoughts and teaching and the development of Christian Science doctrine. In fact, in much of their literature, he comes out as a kind of "pagan" who had some ideas vaguely akin to the truth, but who was not a true believer. The Scientists are indeed fearful of Quimby's influence and of the fact that outsiders credit him with some, or much, of what was to become Christian Science. Yet it is apparent that Phineas P. Quimby, watchmaker, daguerrotypist, and mesmerist, had a profound effect upon Mrs. Patterson and her life and thought.

Hopelessly ill, a perpetual patient, Mary Baker Patterson heard of Quimby and his successes. After much discussion with her sister Abigail (suspicious of Quimby's claims), she went off to

Portland to—perhaps—be cured of chronic illness by this wonder-worker.

Gazing straight into her eyes, Quimby told Mary Baker Patterson that she was held in bondage by her family and her physician. Her animal spirit reflected its grief upon her body and caused her spinal illness. Quimby then wet his hands in a basin of water, rubbed her head, and said he was imparting "healthy electricity" into her. Partly under the spell of the mesmerist, partly due to autosuggestion, Mary Baker Patterson was cured. Radiant, she stood erect. Proud. In fact, shortly she walked up the 182 steps of the tower of the Portland City Hall to see the view.

Daily meetings took place. Quimby thought he had attained one of his most remarkable cures. However, Mrs. Patterson believed that he had merely served as a mediator between herself and God (perhaps that was a later, revisionist report of the conversations). The lively former invalid remained in Portland for three weeks, visiting Quimby daily.

There has been much discussion over this cure. Christian Scientists are certain that Quimby was only an incidental tool in Mrs. Patterson's healing, while her critics believe that she was cured by psychosomatic release as the result of her hypnosis. Whatever happened, she was markedly better if not perfectly cured, and Mrs. Patterson and Quimby entered a relationship that reverberates within Christian Science literature to this day. What part, if any, did Quimby play in the development of what was later to be formal Christian Science? Mary Baker Patterson had definite ideas about the healing power of God, but she was also under the strong influence of Quimby. When she first returned home she used his methods of healing by touch and hypnotism. She wrote, or collaborated upon, or turned over to Quimby her own notes, papers that appeared under his name. To the present, there is controversy over which of his publications were his or Mrs. Patterson's in whole or part.

Back home, Mrs. Patterson suffered a mild relapse. It seemed that Quimby—or God—had not effected a complete cure. But at least she was able to function better than in the past. She still suffered from her spinal troubles, and had chronic indigestion as well. In spite of her physical condition, Mrs. Patterson was impressed by Quimby and his methods, and kept up a regular correspondence with him. She visited him again, in 1864, and to another patient expressed the opinion that "Dr. Quimby is the most progressive magnetic doctor I ever knew, and back of it all there is a science that some day will be discovered." On this visit she spent hours with Quimby each afternoon, and each night wrote down what she had learned, attempting to exhaust the possibilities of his teachings. During the second Quimby period, Mrs. Patterson stayed at several small towns in Maine, tried to get herself healed, and preached Quimby's doctrines to anyone who would listen. When she returned home to her erratic husband, he had moved to Lynn, Massachusetts. Lynn was a prosperous manufacturing town, a center for the shoe industry, and the city had profited immensely from the Civil War because of the Union army's need for footwear. So almost two years passed, to the beginning of 1866. Mrs. Patterson had been maintaining her correspondence with Quimby, but her relationship with him suddenly ended when he died at the end of January. The news is reported to have crushed her, for Quimby had played a major role in her life, and had been, along with her religious beliefs and the Bible, one of the primary sources of her strength. The news of Quimby's death had barely been received when she suffered her fall on the ice.

THE ACCIDENT

During the period immediately after the fall, lying in pain in a strange house, Mrs. Patterson was treated by a well-known doctor, Alvin M. Cushing, who diagnosed "concussion of the brain and spinal dislocation with prolonged unconsciousness and spasmodic seizures." He prescribed a popular medication of the time called the "third decimal attenuation of arnica," which was taken diluted in a glass of water. Mrs. Patterson was unconscious when picked up from the ice, and she remained unconscious throughout the night. Cushing visited his patient twice during that night. In the morning she was semi-conscious and moaning, "Home, home." Cushing gave his patient one-eighth of a grain of morphine. He had carried her to her own home by sleigh, wrapped in fur robes. Cushing again prescribed an attenuation of arnica, which, he learned later, she did not take. On the Sunday morning she experienced her famous revelation and cure after reading about the healing of a palsied man by Jesus.

In this moment, she later recalled, she knew God face to face; she could "touch and handle things unseen." All pain faded into bliss, the discords of her body were transformed into harmony, her sorrow into rapture. God had said to her, "Daughter, arise!"

And she rose. "It was to me a revelation of Truth," she was to write later. "The lost chord of Truth (healing as of Old) I caught consciously from the Divine Harmony. . . . The miracles recorded in the Bible, which before had seemed to me supernatural, grew divinely natural and apprehensible."

Forty years later Cushing declared that he, not God, had cured Mary Baker Patterson with the "third decimal attenuation of arnica." But by that time the doctor was only a minor player in the theological drama that was being played out in Mary Baker Patterson's life. She began to mull over the amazing act of healing she had experienced. It was obviously not a "miracle" but the scientific application of a divine principle—of Christian Science.

Mrs. Patterson had, almost certainly, risen from the dead. More, she had risen on the third day, as Jesus had. From this point on, determined to seek out the principle of live and health which had cured her, she determined to devote her life to that purpose. Like some medieval mystic, she entered a "thorny path" of a "nameless experience." Her husband's reaction to his wife's unworldly decision was a worldly one: He deserted her, leaving Lynn in the company of another woman. Mrs. Patterson writes:

One morning on leaving home, Dr. Patterson said, "You need not expect me back tonight. I have some business and I may be gone for several days." That night he eloped with one of his patients. The husband of the woman, that night returning home, missed his wife, and taking an officer, started in pursuit, found them, and brought his wife home.

The doctor, having lost both wife and paramour, wandered about New England, his practice dwindling, friends rejecting him. In 1873, his wife obtained a divorce from him; he died in Saco, Maine, in the poorhouse, having accepted in full the responsibility for the collapse of his marriage.

For three years Mrs. Patterson was alone, buffeted from town to town, from boarding house to boarding house, living on a meager two hundred dollars a year which Abigail Tilton had persuaded Dr. Patterson to give his abandoned wife.

In the boarding houses at dinner time, surrounded by mill workers and travelers, Mrs. Patterson talked of her cure, of Christ and the science of healing, of the divine laws of "Life, Truth, and Love," which she was working out in her mind. On the third day after her fall she had made a "discovery" that all real being is in God, the divine Mind, that life, Truth, and Love are all-powerful and ever present." On the opposite side is the knowledge that error, sin, sickness, disease, and death are "the false testimony of false material sense, of mind in matter." She added:

My discovery, that erring, mortal, misnamed mind produces all the organism and action of the mortal body, set my thoughts to work in new channels and led to my demonstration of the proposition that Mind is All and matter is naught as the leading factor in Mind science.

"The only realities are the divine Mind and idea," she stated positively. "The divine Principle is demonstrated by healing the sick and is thus proved absolute and divine."

What the many people around the dinner tables thought is not known. Some of them, however, were attracted by her ideas and became her first pupils and followers. If her ideas were correct, then the proof of them was their test by healing disease. She began to cure people, men and women in the boarding houses, neighbors and friends. "I submitted my metaphysical system of treating disease to the broadest practical tests." That is, she began to heal the sick and the ill, the maimed and the dying. Lynn echoed with her success. "That city resounded with my cures," she wrote.

Her patients came from everywhere.

There was a little boy of four and a half with brain fever. "To all appearances the child had ceased to live," she wrote. His mother cried in anguish, "I think he is gone." Mrs. Patterson healed the child. "When I saw his mother coming, I told him to go to the door to meet her."

Mr. John Scott of East Stoughton had no bowel movement for two weeks. Mrs. Patterson found him vomiting, rolling on the floor, and shrieking in agony. He had enteritis as well as stoppage of the bowels. "In less than one hour the pain was entirely gone, the vomiting stopped, and the bowels acted normally," says a description of the cure. The healing was spiritual, too.

A madman broke into Mrs. Patterson's home. He was about to attack her with a chair, but she spoke quietly to him. "Are you from there?" he asked. ("There" is not explained; it could be the heavenly realms or the insane house.) In a few moments the madman was restored to sanity.

A teamster, run over by a heavily laden wagon, his body crushed, was brought into Mrs. Patterson's presence. She went into what seems like spiritual ecstacy ("entirely oblivious of her surroundings," is the description). After a few moments in that state, she noticed that the man had arisen. "Why," he said, "I thought I was hurt, but I am all right."

The crippled, the insane, the helpless invalid "whom Satan hath bound" were all freed by her powers, "powers of love." A consumptive was freed from the prison of her room, an arthritic suddenly walked. And so the cures continued. She had a few converts, among them a young man named Richard Kennedy, with whom she entered into a kind of partnership. Kennedy effected cures while Mrs. Patterson taught. But she went through almost a decade of wandering, rejection, partial acceptance, of praying and healing while what became Christian Science took a definitive form. The partnership with Kennedy failed after two years, but Mrs. Patterson had been able to profit from the experience by a sharpening of her thoughts. In 1875, she progressed to the point where she could afford to buy a house in Lynn, which was hung with a sign saying "Christian Scientists' Home." On June 6 of that year she held her first formal Christian Science service. Meanwhile, after much trouble with printers and publishers, she had brought out the first edition of *Science and Health*, a collection of notes and thoughts which had been worked out for her pupils.

By then her work was solidly established. In 1877, on New Year's Day, she married one of her pupils, the mild-mannered Asa Gilbert Eddy. From that point on she was known as Mary Baker Eddy. Her organization attained a wider following, despite much criticism and even public abuse, and she acquired a firm and staunch nucleus of students and disciples. She had originally been of the mind that she could work through existing churches, propagating her doctrines through established organizations. But opposition on the part of the various Protestant denominations led her to "organize a church designed to commemorate the word and works of our Master, which should reinstate primitive Christianity and its lost element of healing." The Christian Science Association was established in 1876, and in 1879 the Church of Christ (Scientist) was formally chartered, to be followed three years later with the founding of the Massachusetts Metaphysical College. The path was always stormy. There were defections and even lawsuits which harassed her work, but she remained firm to her principles.

Though Christian Science then—as now—was known and noted for its cures, Mrs. Eddy from the beginning tried to emphasize that the major role of her movement was not healing alone but "the coming anew of the Gospel" as promised by Christ. Although . . .

. . . *signs and wonders are wrought in the metaphysical healing of physical disease . . . these signs are only to demonstrate its divine origin,—to attest the reality of the higher mission of the Christ power to take away the sins of the world.*

Nevertheless, the unique healing by Mrs. Eddy and the Christian Scientists was and is a powerful and convincing witness to the truth of the doctrines. There was much popular prejudice against Christian Science, and Mrs. Eddy realized that its truths had to be proven by unquestioned facts. The first edition of *Science and*

Mary Baker Eddy (she was still Mrs. Patterson) at the time she was living in Stoughton, Massachusetts, thinking out the basic principles of Christian Science. It was here, about 1870, that she was working on the manuscript of what was to become her famous *Science and Health.* She married Asa Gilbert Eddy on New Year's Day, 1877, and has been known as Mrs. Eddy since.

Health contained signed testimonies by some of the individuals whom she herself had healed. Most of the people in the early days came to her in desperation, and they told her that Christian Science was recruited from the graveyard, because of the vast number of cases given up for lost by doctors but healed by Mrs. Eddy and her disciples. Whatever the criticisms, by 1880 Lynn seemed too small for the movement, and it was moved to Boston. The same year the National Christian Scientist Association was founded and the next decade showed remarkable growth. It was the period of the founding of several Christian Science publications, and the membership had grown from one congregation of fifty members (who often quarreled not only among themselves but with Mrs. Eddy over doctrines and discipline) to twenty churches and ninety societies in 1890. The church also had thirty-three teaching centers and over two hundred and fifty Christian Science practitioners, men and women who were empowered to heal.

Mrs. Eddy has been much criticized for having taught healing for money. But she had her reasons:

When God impelled me to set a price on my instruction in Christian Science Mind-healing, I could think of no financial equivalent for an impartation of knowledge of that divine power which heals; but I was led to name three hundred dollars as the price for each pupil in one course of lessons at my College,—a startling sum for tuition lasting barely three weeks. This amount greatly troubled me. I shrank from asking it, but was finally led, by a strange providence, to accept this fee. God has shown me, in multitudinous ways, the wisdom of this decision.

However, she did take indigent pupils without tuition, and rhetorically asked of her other students if the lessons were not worth the charge.

Though the movement was expanding with commendable speed, dissenters and heretics continued to plague her, challenging her authority and her doctrines, and even claiming that she—the Discoverer!—was perverting the true science. Lawsuits threatened her, and supposed well-wishers attempted to remove her from her control, ostensibly for her own good. But whatever happened, she was both forceful and kind, practical and saintly, determined and yet flexible in adhering to the doctrines as she understood them. It was Mrs. Eddy alone—despite the ghost of Phineas P. Quimby in the distant background—who had found the divine principles; who shaped the church, the sect; who revealed; who wrote, pronounced, and decided. There are no evangelists, no Saint Paul, no medieval schoolmen—Saint Thomas and Dun Scotus—in Christian Science. What is, came from her own mind. Because of her dominating position, controversy, as well as slight scandal, still surrounds her. When her husband Asa Gilbert Eddy died in 1882, her reputation was shaken to the roots because she had called in a doctor at the last moment. Rumors abounded that Asa Eddy had died of cancer which Mrs. Eddy herself could not cure. Other rumors speculated he had been poisoned. The public believed Mrs. Eddy did not follow her own teachings. The attending doctor performed an autopsy and deduced that Mr. Eddy had died of "heart exhaustion"—that is, a malfunctioning of the valvular structure. Mrs. Eddy's reply about what killed her husband was: "Not material poison but mesmeric poison."

As her fame and success increased, in her later years, Mrs. Eddy was able to withdraw from the daily affairs of the church. In 1892, she "disorganized" the National Christian Science Association; the college was also given up. The Boston church was reorganized as The Mother Church, and Mrs. Eddy still controlled it through twelve charter members and twenty first members and a self-perpetuating board of directors she had appointed. Several editions of *Science and Health* had appeared, the last in 1875, incorporating her final revisions. This is the edition which is in use today. Its pages are standardized, and it contains her "Key" to the Scriptures, which are actually her very special interpretation of the books of Genesis and Revelation. It also includes testimonials to her healing powers, and an analysis of animal magnetism and its associated evils, ending with a glossary of terms which include a capsule of Christian Science beliefs. *Science and Health, with Key to the Scriptures* is the basic Christian Science work, next to the Bible. Its theme is that matter is not real and that only the Divine Mind is real; matter has no life and hence it has no real existence, but Mind is immortal. It is a doctrine that has aided hundreds of thousands, perhaps millions, of people.

In her last years Mrs. Eddy lived in seclusion, saw few people, and took a daily ride in her carriage. Rumors persisted that she was gravely ill, despite the application of the best principles of Christian Science. It was rumored that a double took her place in public. She was forced to hold a news conference for doubting journalists.

The final period of her life was one of difficulty. A coterie of the faithful surrounded her, keeping away enemies, real and imaginary. Until the end she maintained a fear of "the dragon"—malicious animal magnetism, known as MAM. Poor health plagued her; she was given morphine to relieve the pain from kidney stones.

Death came to Mrs. Eddy, as it must to all, in 1910, at the age of ninety. Her death was a special event, for her teachings seemed to have put death beyond the realm of ordinary experience for herself. The word "death" is not used by Christian Scientists about their founder; instead, they speak of the "passing away" of Mrs. Eddy. Various euphemisms are used, for she had stated in *Science and Health* that death is "an illusion, the lie of life in matter, the unreal and the untrue, the opposite of Life," life being God. One biographer stated that Mrs. Eddy "ceased to breathe, passing out of earthly consciousness."

Toward the end of her life she had struggled to define her role, her existence, her own persona. She emphasized that she was "not Jesus," for there was a tendency among the faithful to deify her. At the same time she felt inextricably entwined with the Divine. Her view of herself seemed to place her above and beyond ordinary humans. Often she would remark that "those who look for me in person, or elsewhere than in my writings, lose me instead of finding me." Her associates saw her as the "Comforter" promised by Jesus. A formal statement issued by The Christian Science Board in 1923 and kept in print says:

As Christ Jesus exemplified the fatherhood of God, [*Mrs. Eddy*] *re-*

vealed God's motherhood; she represents in this age the spiritual idea of God typified by the woman in the Apocalypse.

Mrs. Eddy had a life-long fascination with the last book of the New Testament, variously known as the Book of the Apocalypse or the Book of Revelation, chapters twelve and fourteen being especially applicable to herself.

Mrs. Eddy regarded portions of Revelation (that is, Chapter 12) as pointing to her as the one who fulfilled prophecy by giving the full and final revelation of Truth; her work being complementary to that of Christ Jesus.

She was, the board continues, in her own view, the "God-appointed" and "God-anointed" messenger to this age, "the woman chosen by God to discover the Science of Christian healing, and to interpret it to mankind." As a "revelator," she said she would take her proper place in history, "but will not be deified."

When her will was read, it was found that she had acquired an estate of some two million dollars, most of which she left to The Mother Church. Only small amounts went to her son, George Glover, now a mining engineer in the west, and his children. It was a great fortune for a woman who in the worst period of her life had lived on two hundred dollars a year. But her works sold well, and she was hard-headed and businesslike in maintaining copyrights and in making sales.

Christian Science has come under much criticism by outsiders, but it is a doctrine that has had widespread influence on the world, has gained many disciples, and has influenced popular thinking in both religious and secular fields. Like other "American" faiths, it stands as a self-proclaimed, self-evident truth, unique and unassailable. It shows itself as the truth given the world by Christ; the original, the true truth, putting all others into error. Mrs. Eddy had many critics and will have more. Mark Twain called her "a brass god with clay legs." A rival, Mrs. Josephine Curtis Woodbury, in an article written in 1899, called "Quimbyism, or the Paternity of Christian Science," said:

What she has really "discovered" are ways and means of perverting and prostituting the science of healing to her own ecclesiastical aggrandizement, and to the moral and physical depravity of her dupes.

In the long run, Christian Science is a matter of faith to the members of the church and one of questionable value to its critics. Today, in the pressure of newer faiths and the growth of others that also arose in the nineteenth century, Christian Science is slowly losing ground. The church does not issue statistics, but members have expressed concern that the average age of the faithful is older than ever, that the children of believers are leaving, converts are scarce, and that without the forceful presence of the Woman of Revelation—Mrs. Eddy—it cannot maintain its former role.

NEW THOUGHT AND UNITY

Many of the disciples who left Christian Science as heretics, or the disaffected, thought it was too good an idea to be left to the Founder. Others who never joined had the same idea. A number of the lapsed, along with outsiders, founded their own churches, none of which ever equaled the original in strength, numbers, influence, or doctrine. Still, they had and do have their place in the lives of many millions who for various reasons do not choose to enter Mrs. Eddy's grand scheme. Her positive thinking fertilized the entire American scene, always open to onward and upward exhortations. Her concept of a healing ministry has been accepted by many of the more traditional Protestant churches (she never did intend to found a separate organization), and even the more conservative Roman Catholics experiment with it.

Among the first to challenge Mrs. Eddy were Quimbyites, who carried on the old mesmerist's ideas, sometimes turning them into occultism and spiritualism. One of the most prominent was a man named Warren Felt Evans who had been healed by Quimby. Evans, who had been a close friend of Mrs. Eddy's (she had requested him to take over when Quimby died), pushed Quimby's moderate techniques of mesmerism into spiritualism and what he called "esoteric Christianity." His success caused Mrs. Eddy much uneasiness and she resented the competition.

Another Quimbyite was Julius Dresser, who in 1880 began an open controversy with Mrs. Eddy on the matter of their joint master and teacher. Dresser founded a rival organization to Christian Science called the Church of the New Life. Evans and Dresser were part of a movement which came to be called New Thought, and embodied ideas similar to Christian Science. It relied heavily, however, on mesmerism, and challenged and attacked Mrs. Eddy for her dogmatism and authoritarianism. The term "New Thought" gained wide recognition, encompassing several movements. New Thought teachings, as opposed to those of Christian Science, gave great latitude to the individual's freedom. The constitution of the International New Thought Alliance, not published until 1915 (five years after Mrs. Eddy's death), "affirmed" in contrast to Mrs. Eddy's sobriety, an exuberant way of life.

We affirm health . . . we affirm the divine supply [for] within us are unused resources of energy and power. We affirm the new thought of God.

Dozens of other movements arose as apostates from Christian Science began to practice. Some left voluntarily because of differences with the founder or with her followers, or because they finally could not accept the doctrines. Others were excommunicated. Some continued as individual practitioners, while others started their own churches. One of the most important of the disciples to be excommunicated was Augusta Stevens, leader of a prosperous church in Manhattan. Another staunch Christian Scientist was Annie C. Bill, who broke with The Mother Church after Mrs. Eddy's death and established her own Parent Church. It was based upon sound Christian Science principles. But some twenty years later, Mrs. Bill, having developed her own ideas, set forth in her *Science and Reality*, established the Church of the Universal Design.

Another schismatic was Emma Curtiss Hopkins, who founded a rival Christian Science Theological Seminary, which in turn led to still another church. Three sisters in Denver, Alethea

Brooks Small, Fannie Brooks James, and Nona Lovell Brooks, developed principles much like those of Christian Science. Along with Mrs. Malina E. Cramer of San Francisco, who independently had come to the same themes, they joined with Mrs. Hopkins's seminary to produce Divine Science, with headquarters in Denver, and the Religious Science movement in Los Angeles.

The most successful of the rivals has been the Unity School of Christianity. It appeared through the aegis of Mrs. Hopkins, who helped inspire Charles and Myrtle Fillmore. Both were seriously ill, and the husband moreover was bankrupt. Neither was formally a Christian Scientist, though both had studied it, along with New Thought, Quakerism, Theosophy, Rosicrucianism, Spiritism, and Hinduism. They found that the emphasis on the Divine Mind offered the clue that would save man. Founded in 1889, Unity is a formidable rival to Christian Science. It teaches a simplified version of its doctrines, with less emphasis on the negation of matter and more on the latent powers within each person, which must be released through prayer, producing not only peace of mind, inner harmony, and good health, but also worldly success.

"Whatever man wants he can have by voicing his desire in the right way into the Universal Mind," the Fillmores said. All thought goes back to God, who is . . .

. . . *Principle, Law, Being, Mind, Spirit, All Good, omnipotent, omniscient, unchangeable, Creator, Father, Cause and Source of all that is.*

Unity says it is a nonsectarian religious educational institution. "The true church is a state of consciousness in man." In the Unity scheme, things are described with a touch of businesslike organization that appeals to many.

The Father is Principle, the Son is that Principle revealed in a creative plan. The Holy Spirit is the executive power of both Father and Son carrying out the creative plan.

Salvation is to be attained on this earth. Unity teaches that man is a son of God filled with the Christ consciousness, Christ being "Spiritual man . . . the direct offspring of Divine Mind, God's idea of perfect man." It is by means of Christ, the Christ consciousness, that man earns eternal life and salvation. In Unity, salvation is the attainment of that true spiritual body which replaces the physical body when man becomes like Christ. This happens, or can happen, "here on this earth" through a series of reincarnations and regenerations. Man experiences no final death but changes into increasingly better states until he becomes as Christ, in Unity, a state to be shared by all.

In Unity's positive thinking, health is natural, sickness unnatural. Similar ideas apply even to man's economic side, for there, too, man should be healthy. Fillmore once revised the Twenty-third Psalm.

The Lord is my banker; my credit is good. . . .
He giveth me the key to his strongbox;
He restoreth my faith in riches;
He guideth me in the paths of prosperity for His name's sake. . . .

Unity, which is based in Unity Village, Missouri, maintains a constant hotline for people in trouble, or who need prayer. The organization says it receives over ten thousand requests a week by letter, cable, and phone for aid. Each case is assigned to a staff worker and everyone joins in prayer several times a day to help the mass of petitioners. In addition to the prayer vigils, known as Silent Unity, the organization sends out some four million copies of pamphlets, books, tracts, and other literature each year to people who never visit the school. Their names are kept in a vast computerized memory; they are the beneficiaries of faith in the Universal Mind.

5

☆　☆　☆　☆　☆　☆　☆　☆　☆

THE MILLENNIUM: ADVENTISTS AND WITNESSES

A S THE YEAR A.D. 1000 APPROACHED, PEOPLE ALL OVER Christian Europe began to anticipate the millennium—the "thousandth" year since Jesus had been born—and His Second Coming. Churches were refurbished and painted white in anticipation, and as the first day of the year 1000 was welcomed, the populace, dressed in fresh and clean white clothing, flocked to the services. Needless to say, Jesus did not come.

He had been expected before, in the earliest days of the church. After the Resurrection and Ascension, many of His followers believed that He would return soon. In the Gospels and Epistles there were hints that He would come almost immediately ("The time is short," and, "I come quickly"). Yet He did not return. Through the first century His Coming was awaited confidently. By the middle of the second century, however, the church took a more realistic view. It had witnessed at least one disappointment: A Syrian bishop, for example, led his entire flock into the desert to await the Lord; the end of the world did not happen. Both the Latin and Greek churches began to discredit millennial hopes. The fourth-century bishop Saint Augustine said that the church was the kingdom of God and that the millennial kingdom had thus begun with the birth of Jesus. This is a general view held by many traditional Christians, especially those who celebrate the sacrament of communion as the body and blood of Jesus. His Second Coming is manifested daily in the consecrated wine and bread.

Though the major Christian churches discouraged millennial hopes, the idea still held a strong fascination for people submerged in the poverty, cruelty, and chaos of medieval life. Yearnings for the coming of the good Lord Jesus continued to survive. When attacks on the Roman papacy and upon church teachings reached major proportions in the period between the thirteenth and fifteenth centuries, millennialism became an important concept. Among the popular revolutionary movements of the fifteenth and sixteenth centuries—political, economic, and religious—millennialism bloomed in full force. In the sixteenth century, such groups as the Anabaptists tried to establish an ideal, radical, communist Christian society in anticipation of Christ's return.

In the seventeenth century, a group of Russian Orthodox Christians, the Old Believers, became convinced that the end of the world was near. They were called Old Believers because they refused to accept theological and liturgical innovations proposed by the crown and the church hierarchy, and they tried to return to what they thought was the original form of Christianity. They were cruelly persecuted by the tsarist government. Old Believer priests, some of them with unusual charismatic qualities, preached the millennium. Over a period of several years, twenty thousand peasants, dressed in white, either burned themselves or buried themselves alive in the hope of resurrection when Christ came. The Second Coming of a heavenly figure is not solely a Christian hope. The Zoroastrians of Iran await the Second Coming of the Prophet Zoroaster, perhaps in the person of his favorite disciple, Prince Peshotan. Many believe the Prince is waiting for the right time in a cave on sacred Mount Alburz in northern Iran. Numerous Muslim Shi'a sects believe that an imam, or mahdi, will appear to usher in a thousand years of peace. Hindus commonly expect a final incarnation, or avatar, of the god Vishnu who will come to destroy iniquity and restore the age of righteousness, initiating again the beginning of an endlessly repeated cycle. Among the Mahayanist Buddhists, many believe that a form of Gautama Buddha waits in heaven for the time when he will return to earth as the embodiment of love and compassion. And of course the Jews expect a messiah destined to deliver them from their enemies. This hope is not for a Second Coming but for a first, since they did not and could not receive Christ as the Waited One.

Thus the yearning for a heavenly figure, a savior, has run deep in the hearts, minds, and souls of mankind, of whatever age, whatever culture. And even today, not only in certain sects like the various Adventist groups and the Jehovah's Witnesses, but also in many fringe sects, Jesus is expected. Here and there colonies of people have secluded themselves in deserts and on mountain tops, in cities and the countryside, in the momentary expectation of the Second Coming and the end of the world.

Millennialism swept America in the early nineteenth century. It left a legacy of well-established and successful "Second Coming" churches that are among the most popular and powerful of the small sects today. Among the revivalists of Kentucky and Tennessee at the turn of the century there was a firm belief that Jesus would come in the summer of 1805, when He would begin His reign on earth and sin would end. Great excitement was noted among the faithful, but the summer of 1805 passed, and then the year, without God's visible presence. Millenarianism, though temporarily set back, did not die. The mood was too powerful, the expectation too deep, the yearnings too great to be defeated by one such disappointment. A miscalculation, perhaps? A misreading of the sacred texts? Scholars, clergy, and the laity reapplied themselves to a more intense, more thoughtful examination of the Bible.

One of the most important—and most explicit—passages for the millennialists is found in Revelation 20:1–6, which describes how an angel descended to bind the ancient serpent who is the Devil and Satan, to throw him bound into a pit for a thousand years. Then the "souls of them that were beheaded" for Christ came to life, and reigned with him "a thousand years." The others of the dead were not given life until the thousand years had passed. When the saints and the Lord have reigned, the text says, Satan will be released and a great battle—Armageddon—will take place.

Such a text in its literal sense, as well as other passages in Revelation, in various Epistles, in Ezra 4 and in Daniel, have laid the basis for millennial hopes. Some biblical scholars, however, for example in referring to Revelation 20:1–6, have said, "One must beware of reading more into this passage than is warranted; e.g., nothing is said here about a reign on earth." And the Shakers, more simplistic and otherworldly, said the Second Coming, in the form of Mother Ann, was manifested in the individual within.

But fervor won over caution despite the long history of failures. Between 1820 and 1830 some three hundred priests of the Church of England, along with hundreds of nonconformist ministers and preachers, publicly advocated the belief that the Second Coming was near. On the Continent, biblical scholars, priests, and ministers also came to the same conclusion. The United States was not far behind, and it soon led the rest of the Christian world in proclaiming the Second Coming. Presbyterians, Baptists, Congregationalists, Episcopalians, and Methodists—the "established" churches of the nation—took up the belief.

One of the most active investigators of the prophetical texts was a young farmer named William Miller, who lived in upstate New York, near the Vermont border. Miller, though relatively uneducated, was a diligent student of the Bible. Originally a vague nonbeliever, Miller became converted to the Baptists in 1816 and began a detailed study of the Scriptures. The prophecies of Daniel and Revelation especially intrigued him. Miller worked primarily with the King James Bible and a Concordance, making marginal notes, to understand the prophecies that he believed were soon to reach fulfillment. Like other more educated and traditional biblical scholars, Miller came to the conclusion that the "day" of the biblical prophecy was a symbol for a year. Thus he figured that the two thousand three hundred days of Daniel 8:14 started concurrently with the seventy years of Daniel 9, which was in fact the calendar year 457 B.C. The two periods do not end at the same time, so Miller took the longer (the other already having been completed) as the more significant. This brought him to the year A.D. 1843. He also decided that the "sanctuary" mentioned in Daniel 8:14 was either the earth or the church. Whatever the object, it would be purified by flames at the Second Coming, which he firmly and confidently established would take place between March 21, 1843, and March 21, 1844. "God in His wisdom has so interwoven the several prophecies," said Miller, that "they tell us the same things."

By 1828, he had reached the point where he felt a "call" to inform the world that Jesus would return "about 1843." Yet he lacked the confidence to speak publicly. "I tried to excuse myself," he was to explain. "I told the Lord that I was not used to speaking . . . that I was slow of speech and slow of tongue. But I could get no relief." The call bore down on him incessantly, and he began to talk of the millennium to friends and neighbors. In 1831, he was invited to speak at a local church. To his surprise he suddenly became eloquent on the subject of the Second Coming. Other invitations came, and shortly he found himself famous—or notorious, depending on how seriously one took his interpretations. He soon became known nationally. He put his computations and theories together in a book *Evidence from Scripture and History of the Second Coming of Christ about the Year 1843.*

The time was ripe for any belief that would make sense in a crumbling world. The 1830s were ravaged by severe social and economic problems in the young republic, a sign to the faithful of the coming millennium. Martin Van Buren, a protégé of Andrew Jackson, was inaugurated president in 1837, and shortly afterward a nationwide depression—the Panic of 1837—began. The depression lasted three years. Meanwhile the unemployed roamed the streets and banks failed. People begged and slept wherever they could, in doorways and hovels and alleys. At the same time there was a number of fiscal scandals. In one of the worst, the Collector of the Port of New York absconded with over one million two hundred and fifty dollars in government funds—a very large sum now, but almost unheard of then. Everything pointed to the probability of the millennium.

Miller might have been remembered as but one of several millennialists had it not been for his discovery. In 1839, a prominent minister, Josiah V. Hines, a thirty-four-year-old entrepreneur, heard Miller on a speaking tour in New Hampshire. He immediately offered to become his manager and publicity agent. Hines, a fast-talking Bostonian, saw the potential in Miller's message (it is not at all clear if Hines believed in it), and he put the simple and plain farmer on a professional basis, equipping him with a tent and drawing up elaborate charts outlining the prophecies and their course. Hines also began a series of publications, including monthly magazines in various cities, and recruited other, more skilled, evangelists to preach. He sent his teams out on speaking tours and to camp meetings and revivals. Besides periodicals such as *Midnight Cry*, *Signs of the Times*, and *Trumpet of Alarm*, the publications included children's books, catechisms, tracts, pamphlets, and a hymn book, *The Millennial Harp*.

Millennial fever swept the nation, particularly along the eastern coast. Tens of thousands—probably fifty thousand to one hundred thousand—were confirmed believers, and perhaps a million were uneasily expectant. As the fateful year approached, more and more converts were made, the greatest number coming from the Free Will Baptists. The appearance of a comet early in 1844 seemed proof that the End of Time was near. Many people sold or gave away their possessions and their homes, for in the millennium earthly goods would be valueless. Some of the faithful went to the tops of moutains so as to be nearer to heaven when the Lord appeared.

But Jesus did not come on March 21, 1843, nor did He

come during the remainder of the year, nor in the first three
months of 1844. Miller publicly confessed his disappointment and
chagrin. But there was still hope. Some of his followers pointed out
that there obviously was to be a "tarrying time." According to Lev-
iticus 25:9 and Habakkuk 2:3, a leeway of seven months and ten
days was allowed, thus bringing the Lord's coming to October 22,
1844. The cry of "the Tenth Day of the Seventh Month" rallied the
more fervent believers. Miller himself, who had been initially
skeptical, was converted to the new date. "I see a glory in the seventh month which I never saw before. Thank the Lord, O my soul!"
he said. "I am almost home. Glory! Glory! Glory! I see that the time
is correct." Though some had dropped out, the delay brought in
fresh numbers of converts.

But again the people were disappointed, the Lord did not
come, and the episode became known as the Great Disappointment. Much bitterness and disillusionment ensued. A few people
became Shakers, and that was the last major influx into that movement. Miller was excommunicated by his own church, the Baptists,
and died a forlorn and unhappy man in 1849. He was discredited
and virtually forgotten, except by the groups that revised his work,
or by the historians, who see Miller's millennialism as a prime example of American lunacy at its most interesting.

THE ADVENTISTS

Miller had failed; his followers were disappointed. There was
much scoffing and ridicule among the more orthodox Christians,
as among those who professed no faith at all. Still there remained
small groups of people, now scattered and isolated, who continued
to believe that Jesus would come, sooner rather than later. The
problem was, they insisted, in errors in calculation and in misreading the sacred texts. Meeting the year after the Great Disappointment, a small group of Millerites convened in Albany to try to discuss the situation and to work on the texts. They were convinced
that the problem was one of misinterpretation.

Miller had shown the way and had been the rallying point
around which millennialist beliefs could coalesce. The focus

shifted to an unusual young woman, Ellen Gould Harmon, born November 26, 1827, in Gorham, Maine. She and a twin sister, Elizabeth, had been the last of eight children. The parents were Methodists. In 1840, the Harmon family attended one of William Miller's meetings in Portland and was converted. They stood firm in millennialism, even though the Methodist church expelled Robert Harmon and six of his children in 1843 for their beliefs. Ellen, then sixteen, was one of those to be dropped from the church rolls. The Great Disappointment ended the Harmons' faith in millennialism, except for Ellen, who remained convinced.

Less than two months after the last, disappointing day for William Miller's followers, Ellen Harmon had a vision. The date was in December 1844, and she had just passed her seventeenth birthday a few weeks earlier. She visited one of her Adventist friends; one morning the women of the family gathered around the family altar.

It was not an exciting occasion [said Ellen Gould Harmon later], *and there were but five of us present, all women. While I was praying, the power of God came upon me as I had never felt it before. I was wrapped in a vision of God's glory. . . .*

At this time I had a view of the experience of the advent believers, the coming of Christ, and the reward to be given to the faithful.

What this vision was is as remarkable as anything ever experienced by a biblical prophet or a medieval mystic. She was shown:

. . . the advent people traveling on an elevated road to heaven, with a brilliant light illuminating the pathway. At the end of this path was the golden City of God, the New Jerusalem described by John in the last chapter of Revelation. The light shining from the commencement of the trail was symbolic of the Lord's presence with the movement from its beginning until the second coming of the Lord.

This was but the first of a series of visions of exceptional character and quality. She had a second vision about a week after the first, when . . .

. . . *the Lord gave me a view of the trials through which I must pass, and told me that I must go and relate to others what He had revealed to me. It was shown me that my labors would meet with great opposition, and that my heart would be rent with anguish; but that the grace of God would be sufficient to sustain me through all.*

The call was clear but Ellen was "exceedingly troubled." An angel had spoken to her directly, but she prayed that someone else might be given the burden of making God's message public. "I coveted death," she later wrote, "as a release from the responsibilities that were crowding upon me." She was still in her teens, in poor health, in "constant bodily suffering, and to all appearances had but a short time to live." She was timid, retiring, and unable to talk to strangers. She feared, also, that if she did go forth as the angel commanded, the honor and responsibility of one favored from the Most High with visions and revelations would make her vain and exalted. Finally she submitted to the Lord, ready to follow His commands.

By 1915, she had experienced some two thousand prophetic visions and dreams. She denied that she was a "prophetess" and said she was nothing but "a messenger, sent to bear a message from the Lord to his people." Her disciples, the group now called the Seventh-day Adventists, claimed she was indeed divinely inspired, proof being that her "teachings and admonitions are in harmony with the Scriptures," and that "through her were revealed secrets that only God could bring to light," and most importantly, "predictions made by her regarding future events came to pass as foretold."

The Albany meeting of 1845 soon broke up into three groups, each convinced that it alone had the key to the millennium and could explain the reason for Christ's failure to appear according to prophecy. The small group that gathered near Washington, New Hampshire, of which Ellen Gould Harmon was a key mem-

Ellen Gould White was the guiding light and revelator of doctrine of the Seventh-day Adventists from her late teens until her death in 1915 at the age of eighty-eight.

ber, was convinced that the date of October 22, 1844, was indeed correct, but that Jesus had not appeared because of a neglect of Sabbath observances by the faithful. They said that the seventh day, Saturday (not the first day of the week, Sunday), was the true Sabbath. This was a theme picked up from the Seventh Day Baptists, an English sect which was a survival of the Fifth Monarchy Men. (The Seventh Day Baptists, German, are an unrelated group, who trace their origin back to the Ephrata Society, and are affiliated with the Dunkards.)

But most important of all was the interpretation of what Jesus was to do, and where. Using Daniel 8:13–14 as the key, the group decided that Jesus was not to come out of but to *enter into* the Most Holy Place in heaven in order to complete the second stage of His priestly ministry. In 1846, this doctrine, including that of seventh-day worship, was published by one of the New Hampshire group, a man named Joseph Bates, and it received wide publicity. Shortly after that Ellen Gould Harmon married a fellow believer, James White, and since then has been known in Adventist circles as Ellen Gould White.

The group began a series of publications emphasizing the coming of Jesus and the necessity of the correct Sabbath, spending all their limited funds on the effort. Mrs. White, her husband James, and Bates wrote and spoke in terms that Adventists today hold "in highest esteem," accepting their works as "inspired counsels from the Lord." Suffering severe financial handicaps at first, the group faced both privation in the lonely way of life they had chosen and ridicule for the failure of past messianic expectations. But disciples came and in 1855 the Whites and Bates and their followers moved to Battle Creek, Michigan, and five years later formally incorporated themselves as the Seventh-day Adventists.

Meanwhile other Adventist groups, all descendants of the Miller movement, were organized. They differed from each other in interpretation of Scriptures and traditional Christian beliefs. The same year as the Battle Creek conference, the Advent Christian Church was formed in Salem, Massachusetts, with the doctrine of a sometime everlasting kingdom of God upon earth, and an unusual view of the fate of the human soul. One of the group's leaders,

Jonathan Cummings, stated that immortality was a gift from Christ for a certain few chosen at the Resurrection. Until then there would be "conditional immortality," in which all the dead would remain unconscious; they would be judged by a divine tribunal for either rewards or punishments, and in the heavenly kingdom on earth all evil would be exterminated. Several smaller Adventist groups banded together along with sects of English immigrant Adventists in 1888. They went through several reorganizations under various names, including the Church of God Jesus Christ. They are now called the Church of God General Conference. They believe that the kingdom of God will be literal and will be founded by Jesus at Jerusalem and will spread throughout the world. The dead will sleep until the Resurrection, when the righteous will awaken to eternal life and the wicked will suffer a second death.

Most Adventists today are members of the Seventh-day church. Despite a schism led by an Elder Cranmer (The Church of God, Adventist) in protest against the claimed divine inspiration of Ellen Gould White, it has remained the major and most successful body of believers.

The church's headquarters were moved from Battle Creek to Washington, D.C., in 1903, where they have remained since. They send out missionaries all over the world to prepare people of all races and beliefs for the Second Coming, an effort which has met with considerable success. By the end of the 1970s, formal membership in the Seventh-day Adventists was close to 2.5 million, about a fifth of that number in the United States and Canada. Some four thousand churches are counted. Another 3.5 million to 4 million people, young and old, attend Adventist Sabbath schools weekly, and almost forty thousand missionaries are abroad, working in every nation (including the Soviet Union) and preaching in over five hundred languages.

Adventists call themselves "Bible loving," and they center their lives on a literal interpretation. It is the Bible through which they define the world and predict the future. They "eschew priest, saint, or other ecclesiastical functionary," preferring direct prayer. The Adventists believe that their church is not an inventor of new doctrines but a discoverer of ancient truths long eclipsed by the infiltration of pagan superstitions and customs into Christianity. And at every moment there is the expectation of the imminent return of Jesus. The Adventist "lives under a sense of destiny, believing that it is his duty to warn mankind that the end of the world is at hand," explains an Adventist spokesman.

THE JEHOVAH'S WITNESSES

About three decades after William Miller's Great Disappointment, a young Pennsylvanian, Charles T. Russell, a haberdasher of the small town of Allegheny and a member of the local Congregational church, began to have doubts about the truths of the Bible. Then he came across an Adventist preacher— "stumbled" was the word Russell used—and his "wavering faith" was sent into a new direction. The belief that Christ would return—a doctrine not stressed by the Congregationalists—became basic to his thinking. Russell began to study the Scriptures in depth.

His Adventist contact, N. H. Barbour, as the result of his own studies, had decided that the key word "coming" in Matthew 24:27, 37, and 39 in the standard King James Bible was better translated as "presence" in the Diaglott Bible published by a man named Benjamin Wilson. After some correspondence, Russell and Barbour got together and began to talk over the situation. Together they began a magazine called *The Herald of the Morning*, which stressed their discovery that the presence of Jesus was "invisible." Russell and Barbour had a falling out over the doctrine of the atonement, and Russell, after much introspection, decided that he would have to carry on the work according to his own interpretation. With a small group of followers, he established what was to be the key organ of his work, *The Watch Tower and Herald of Christ's Presence*. It has survived to the present, with minor changes in title (it is now called *The Watchtower Announcing Jehovah's Kingdom*).

The central teaching that Russell established was that the invisible Second Coming of Jesus had happened in the autumn of 1874. This date marked the start of the Millennial Age, the "Day of Jehovah," which, Russell told the world, was foreshadowed by an international revolution of the working classes that brought the world to chaos. At the same time he began to stress that God should be called Jehovah. However, the movement was not formally known as "Jehovah's Witnesses" until 1931. Up to that time it had a variety of names—Russellites, Millennial Dawnists, International Bible Students, and Rutherfordites.

Despite the date of 1874 for the invisible return of Jesus, a second date, that of 1914, was set for His *visible* return. This, Russell said, was to be the year when "the kingdoms of this world" would come to an end, and "the full establishment of the Kingdom of God will be accomplished." Like William Miller, three-quarters of a century earlier, Russell had put a very individual and special interpretation on biblical texts. Drawing upon a passage in Saint Luke 21:24 referring to "the appointed times of the nations," Russell postulated the question, "Gentile Times: When Do they End?" in an article in 1876. The answer was: "The seven times will end in A.D. 1914." All of this is very obscure to most who consult their Bibles, but Russell convinced a fair number of people that Jesus was coming in 1914 and the millennium would then begin. His followers were fervent and avid proselytizers of the message of Christ's return; millions of copies of millennial publications flooded the country. In 1912, Russell constructed a "Photo-Drama of Creation," using motion pictures and his own ingenious soundtrack to show the period from the creation of the earth—4026 B.C. in his calculations—to the imminent return of Jesus in 1914 and His thousand-year reign.

As in the failure of the Millerites' and other millennialists' predictions, Jesus did not return to earth. The forewarned year passed without heavenly intervention. However, World War I broke out; to Russell this was partial confirmation of his belief that universal chaos was upon mankind. His re-examination of Scripture proved to him that Christ's return had indeed taken place in 1914. The Lord, Russell decided, was ruling from a new place in heaven, sitting on the right hand of God the Father. How Russell was able to make this deduction has never been clear to critics of his doctrines, but the faithful accept it without question. Wars, earthquakes, famines, pestilence, increasing lawlessness, social chaos—

the common lot of most of the world—confirmed to Russell the "end of Gentile times and the beginning of the transition period from human rule to the thousand-year reign of Christ." War in heaven would lead to "Satan's being cast to earth, woe on earth, and Christ would rule in the midst of his enemies for a period not exceeding one generation." The complete end of world wickedness would come through a "great tribulation," culminating in a war at Har-Magedon (or Armageddon) followed by Christ's thousand-year reign of peace. A selected and limited number of the saved—144,000, according to the Witnesses' interpretation of the Book of Revelation—will go to heaven; the less fortunate of the saved "will live forever on earth"—"a cleansed and beautiful earth" which "will never become boring." Death will be no more.

Russell, despite his religious beliefs and his calls to the world to repent, was not free from human fallibilities. He and his wife had a falling out in the 1890s, and she sued for divorce. The situation was scandalous, and Russell's enemies—of whom there were many—made the most of the situation. During this period there were several defections from his group, with much anger over his authoritarian methods of control. However, Russell survived the challenges, though the millennialist movement did not grow significantly during this period. He died in 1916 at the age of sixty-four.

The next year, after a bitter struggle among the high command, Missouri-born Judge Joseph F. Rutherford was elected second president of the Zion Watch Tower Tract Society, as the group was called at the time. The new leader was an able, aggressive, dynamic lawyer, who had defended Russell in the divorce hearings. He began to develop his own views of the coming millennium. He replaced Russell's writings with his own and leaned heavily upon the slogan "Many now living will never die." Rutherford's interpretations were accepted with great difficulty by the faithful, for Russell had firmly built up an imposing view of his own role. Taking his text from the New Testament passage about the "faithful and wise servant" whom the Lord had made ruler over his household, Russell had seen his mission in almost messianic and divine terms. Most of his followers accepted that interpretation; dissenters were forced from the Society. Thus the faithful believed that all the truth

God had seen fit to reveal to His people had been revealed to Russell and nothing more could be brought forth because the "servant" was dead.

But Rutherford quickly forced his views upon the faithful, and the movement began to grow more rapidly than it had under its founder. The judge led his people into radical positions, which they have maintained quite courageously and firmly ever since. Because the Witnesses were sure that worldly governments were not Christian, they refused to salute the flag (so as not to put secular symbols ahead of God's) and they would not support the war effort, for by 1917 the United States was deeply involved in the hostilities with Germany and the Central Powers. Rutherford and seven others were arrested and tried for "the offense of unlawfully, feloniously and willfully causing insubordination, disloyalty and refusal of duty in the military and naval forces of the United States of America when the United States was at war." Rutherford received eighty years, and the others lesser terms. All were released when the war ended.

After this came a period of rapid growth for the movement. Rutherford used the latest and newest technological techniques. Not only did publications by the millions appear, but he made recordings of his doctrines, which were carried from house to house by his people and played on portable phonographs. In 1924, the Society inaugurated the first noncommercial radio station, WBBR in New York City, and 5 other stations were soon opened. The Society also broadcast internationally over another 408 commercial radio stations. Witness use of the airwaves brought them into numerous battles. In Philadelphia, for example, the chancery office of the Roman Catholic archdiocese threatened a boycott of the owners of station WIP for an intended broadcast by Rutherford. They charged that he "attacks the Catholic Church, misrepresents her teachings & foments religious hatred and bigotry." The owners—Gimbel Brothers—backed down and were sued by the Witnesses. Despite several petitions in favor of the Witnesses, one signed by 2.6 million people, and the efforts of their lawyers, the matter was never settled legally, and the next year Rutherford withdrew from all commercial broadcasts.

Whatever the issues involved in the radio broadcasts, the

Witnesses charged that both the Roman Catholic and the various Protestant churches "are conspicuous by their arrogance, self-conceit, impiety and ungodliness." The established churches, along with the "political and commercial powers, science and philosophy," the Witnesses believed, were in "Satan's world." Only the "appointed"—the Witnesses—responded to . . .

. . .Jehovah's direction of his anointed and spirit-begotten witnesses to whom he had specifically given the commission to root out and tear down false doctrine. . . . The anointed of Jehovah [stand] out alone on earth against Satan's entire organization.

Taking on the entire world, secular and ecclesiastical alike, is not an easy task. The Jehovah's Witnesses, convinced in their godly mission, persisted, and the membership of the Society continued to grow. Members went out all over the world, using the latest technology: Sound cars were an innovation in the ministry, employed in teams. The aggressive nature of the Witness missionaries—called "publishers"—often brought arrests for various reasons, such as disturbing the peace and similar minor charges. When a Witness was brought to the local jail, he would phone his headquarters, and in a matter of minutes dozens if not hundreds of Witnesses would converge on the prison, with lists of all the other Witnesses in the area in case the police wanted mass arrests. Such techniques usually made it clear to the authorities that harassing the Witnesses was a losing policy, and it gained them much publicity.

This arrangement [says a Witness publication] made it possible to overwhelm the opposers by sheer numbers so that, no matter how "hot" the territory was, practically every house was reached with the good news of the Kingdom.

When World War II came in 1941 with the Japanese attack on Pearl Harbor, the Witnesses were unalterably opposed to taking part in America's battle, since they saw it as one more sign of Satan's activities. Witnesses had already suffered in Europe for refusing to participate in the fighting. Some had died in Nazi camps,

At an annual convention in New York's Shea Stadium, a young woman is baptized into the Jehovah's Witnesses. The movement often draws tens of thousands of members from around the world to its yearly meetings, and may receive hundreds, and sometimes thousands, of new members at each convention.

and the Allied powers had imprisoned others for refusing to fight. In the United States, Witnesses claimed exemption as conscientious objectors, and they had to fight over and over again in the courts. In a number of local battles, the children of Witnesses refused to salute the American flag, again with court cases, at first decided against the Witnesses, with the Supreme Court ruling at last in support of their claim to religious freedom. Their right to distribute religious literature went through court battles also, with the Witnesses, after many struggles, again vindicated.

Rutherford died in 1942, in the midst of a time of tension for the Witnesses as they fought to practice their very unpopular doctrines in the midst of heavy pressure to conform during the American war effort. The new president, Nathan H. Knorr, was a long-time Witness, but he was not president of the Jehovah's Witnesses as such but of the two Watch Tower Bible and Tract Societies (Pennsylvania and New York) and of the International Bible Students Association. Born in 1905, Knorr joined the Society at the age of sixteen in Allentown, Pennsylvania, and worked his way up through the Society. Under Knorr the work continued, perhaps less flamboyantly, but quietly aggressively, and dedicated to the belief that world conditions quite pointedly proved the Witnesses' belief that the Second Coming of Jesus was close at hand.

Surely the continued wars, droughts, famines, earthquakes, revolutions, depressions, social chaos, rising crime, drug addiction, sexual promiscuity, and pornography helped fortify the claims of all the various millennialists, of whatever type. And such additional modern horrors as engines falling out of airplanes, motors dropping out of subway cars, and the metallic rain of abandoned, disintegrating spacecraft heighten the widespread apprehension shared by people around the world ready to accept millennial doctrines.

The Last Days are upon us, say Adventists and Witnesses alike, and Jesus will soon come to rule, and to separate the anointed from the damned, in a New Jerusalem of a thousand years.

6

HOLINESS
AND
PENTECOSTALISM

THEY SPEAK WITH TONGUES AND THEY CURE BY FAITH, but most of all they are visited by the Holy Spirit, according to Acts 2:2–4, when the followers of Jesus assembled in Jerusalem on the feast of Pentecost . . .

And suddenly there came a sound from heaven as of a rushing mighty wind, and it filled all the house where they were sitting.

And there appeared unto them cloven tongues like as of fire, and it sat upon each of them.

And they were all filled with the Holy Ghost, and began to speak with other tongues, as the Spirit gave them utterance.

What happened in the first day of the church, the Pentecostals believe, happens again and again to them. The vast movement known as Pentecostalism, which encompasses hundreds of denominations and millions of believers, is the fastest-growing of all forms of Christianity.

Pentecostalism is not a new phenomenon, though its current expression came to maturity in the 1960s upon roots that can be traced back to the great revivals in Kentucky and Tennessee in the first decade of the nineteenth century, and revived in the 1880s and 1890s. Pentecostalism, and its earlier and related form of "Holiness," is based upon the power of the Holy Spirit to enliven and sanctify the believer. Tending to withdraw from the mundane world and from mainstream Protestantism (and Catholicism), the Pentecostals give an eloquent and charismatic witness to the fact that they have been "seized," just as the first disciples were, by the breath, the fire, of the Third Person of the Trinity. In fact, among some Pentecostals the Trinity turns into a Duo, for God the Father is ignored and forgotten in the redeeming Love of Jesus and the infusion of the Holy Spirit. This "baptism of the Spirit" has touched millions, who find themselves speaking in tongues, practicing the gift of healing (though traditional medicine is usually not eschewed), and gaining illumination through ecstatic mass singing and chanting, and even dancing.

Pentecostalism has flourished and waned and flourished again throughout the life of Christianity. Its signs can be seen wherever believers place exceptional emphasis on the power of the Holy Spirit. The French Camisards, who influenced the Shaking Quakers, the first Quakers themselves, the early Methodists, the Jumpers, Ranters, Fifth Monarchy Men, numerous Anabaptists, the Shakers—all showed Pentecostal manifestations.

The revivalists of the early American frontier meetings are good examples of Pentecostal enthusiasm. The kind of frontier people who attended the revivals, many of them outcasts, poor, downtrodden, and uneducated, brought about the founding of dozens of new small churches. Many of these people, who felt outside the mainstream of American life, also came to believe that the established churches—the Methodists, Presbyterians, Episcopalians, and even the numerous Baptist groups—represented rank and privilege and not the common people. Others were disturbed by the theological, doctrinal, and liturgical innovations that were creeping into the larger churches, and they sought a return to "fundamentals," with a strong emphasis on the literal truth of the Bible. That the Bible contained all that man needed to know and that the Holy Scriptures were without error—and not to be interpreted broadly, poetically, or metaphorically—was a doctrine essential to fundamentalist belief and practice. From among these various dissenters was born a diverse group of churches outside the center of American religious life.

An urge for "sanctification" in the Holy Spirit led to the growth of what became known as the Holiness churches, and then, going further in the Spirit, to the groups generally labeled "Pentecostals," who believe not only in baptism in the Spirit but usually in fundamentalism and the inerrancy of the Bible. These churches give visible and audible charismatic testimony of the inner illumination they have received, showing signs of ecstatic states such as chanting, shouting, or talking in tongues.

In the period before the Civil War, the question of slavery had divided many denominations, especially the Methodists. Churches often fell into Northern and Southern sections. Shortly before the war, the Methodists had experienced a "Holiness" revival, which was sparked by a re-examination of John Wesley's doctrines. Wesley, who had begun the movement that came to be called "Methodism," had believed that some Christians, through God's grace, would experience "perfectionism," the complete realization of moral or spiritual possibilities in personal experience. Or, he believed, they would undergo complete sanctification in this life as the culminating event in spiritual development. After the Civil War ended in 1865, a "Holiness Revival" continued among Methodists, and in 1867, a Holiness camp meeting in Vineland, New Jersey, produced such dramatic results that a National Camp

Meeting Association for the Promotion of Holiness was formed. Holiness began to spread among Methodists, though it was rejected by members of more conventional churches. Soon Holiness was taken up by Christians outside the Methodist churches, and Holiness became a separate religious movement.

Similar forms of belief also may have arisen spontaneously among people in the former frontier areas. Around the 1880s and 1890s, small groups of Christians in the Midwest and the South, dissatisfied with the mainline churches, began to come together to seek new ways of worshiping and searching for the fundamentals of Christianity they believed had been lost in the established churches. The histories of these churches are very unclear: Often dissimilar bodies had similar names; some changed names every few years. One of the key groups was organized in 1886 in Monroe County, Tennessee, under the direction of Richard G. Spurling. As a Christian fellowship, it was first called the Christian Union, then it was formally known as the Holiness Church, and then it took the name of Church of God. (These names are confusing, for there are now dozens of Holiness churches and several hundred Churches of God, each independent of the other.)

The freedom that ensued from baptism in the Spirit led to different interpretations of what Holiness was and how it was to be practiced. A group of Spurling's people broke away and established what was known as the (Original) Church of God, and soon other such churches were also founded. One of the more common church names is "Fire Baptized," signifying the tongues of flame of the Holy Spirit. In 1890, in southeast Kansas, a group calling itself the Fire-Baptized Holiness Church Association was formed by dissenters from Methodism. However, their doctrine was primitive Wesleyan, emphasizing sanctification in the Holy Spirit and complete holiness. In 1908, most of the black members of the church broke away to form the Fire Baptized Holiness Church, which was even more Pentecostal in tone, and still teaches the standard Holiness and Pentecostal doctrines of repentance, regeneration, justification and sanctification, Pentecostal baptism, speaking in tongues, divine healing, and the Second Coming of Jesus. As so often happens, this small group suffered a schism. In 1911, arguments over matters of discipline (such as the wearing of jewelry and the type of clothing) brought about the founding of the Pentecostal Fire-Baptized Holiness Church. All of these splinter groups are small, with memberships estimated at less than one thousand per organization, but they are witness to the Pentecostal spirit.

After the 1890s, Pentecostalism spread with a great surge, from the old antebellum states of the Deep South, to the Great Plains, to Texas and California, and back. One of the most significant events in the growth of Pentecostalism occurred at Topeka, Kansas, where on January 1, 1900, the gift of the Holy Spirit came to a young woman, Agnes N. Ozman, at Bethel Bible College. Bethel's founder was Charles F. Parham, a prominent Holiness preacher, who claimed the gift of divine healing. The grace that visited Miss Ozman quickly came upon other students at Bethel; they began to speak in tongues and show other Pentecostal signs. (Critics suggested that it was a form of mass hysteria, but believers thought otherwise.) By 1903, Bethel's young people were talking openly about their experiences, and the news of baptism in the Holy Spirit spread from coast to coast. For a while it was known as the Latter Rain Movement, a term derived from the "former rain" and "latter rain" of Joel 2:23.

Be glad, then, ye children of Zion, and rejoice in the Lord your God: for he hath given you the former rain moderately, and he will cause to come down for you the rain, the former rain, and the latter rain in the first month.

Fundamentalist Holiness and Pentecostalists took this phrase with an active stretch of the imagination to refer to the speaking in tongues of Pentecost in Acts 2:4 and of the descent of the Holy Spirit immediately before the premillennial return of Jesus.

Texas was one of the first recipients of the Latter Rain, and quickly it reached the West Coast. In 1906, the Azuza Street Mission in Los Angeles became a Pentecostal center under the leadership of the great black minister, William J. Seymour. The Azuza Pentecostals brought the new message back to the East Coast, where the seeds had already been sown among the existing Holiness churches. From then on, it seemed to be accepted everywhere, not only among the Holiness sects but now among people previously resistant to Holiness doctrines, in particular the Baptists. Not only was the message of the outpouring of the Holy Spirit attractive, but so were speaking in tongues and divine healing, for many people distrusted doctors and relied upon folk nostrums and patent medicines. An extremely puritanical code of dress and behavior also marked Pentecostalism. And, the Pentecostals were theological conservatives, believing in the infallibility of the Bible. That the Holy Spirit was freely descending upon them was taken as a sign that the Last Days were approaching, and that Jesus would return.

One of the key figures during this period was a young man named A. J. Tomlinson. He was a colporteur, or Bible salesman, for the American Bible Society. He joined the Church of God in 1903, which had previously been known as the Holiness Church and had parishes in Tennessee and other border states. In 1908, Tomlinson received baptism in the Holy Spirit and began to spread Pentecostalism among the churches in the South, working particularly among Baptists, who so far had been touched only peripherally by the movement. Tomlinson was an energetic but controversial person. Five of the bodies which call themselves the Church of God can claim descent from his work. Arguments among church members brought Tomlinson's impeachment in 1923, and he withdrew from the Church of God to form the Tomlinson Church of God. (In 1953, the name was changed to the Church of God in Prophecy.) When Tomlinson died in 1943, the Church was divided between his two sons: Milton, who remained at the church headquarters in Cleveland, Tennessee, and Homer, who organized his portion in Queens Village, New York, calling it simply the Church of God. The Cleveland group suffered a schism and, in 1957, the Church of God of all Nations was formed by the dissenters.

In the first decade of this century, the Latter Rain movement—Pentecostalism—was so widespread that it could afford to send missionaries abroad. It also was inevitable that the diffuse churches would be organized into one body. In April 1914, under the leadership of Eudorus N. Bell, some three hundred delegates from all over the nation met at Hot Springs, Arkansas, to try to unify the churches. The result was the fellowship called the Assemblies of God, but it failed to gather all Pentecostals under one roof. While the mainly white churches were organizing, the blacks also came together to form their own Assembly.

Today, the Assembly of God is the largest of all Pentecostal groups, with over a million members, numerous foreign missions, weekly and monthly periodicals, publishing houses, colleges and Bible institutes, and television and radio broadcasts on an international scale (some 630 stations). The various Assemblies officially stand against war, but their young men may accept noncombatant status, and some have served as combatants in the nation's wars.

SHOWMAN EVANGELISM

Pentecostalism was helped to national fame with the appearance of the dynamic woman known as Aimee Semple McPherson, who was born in Ontario, Canada, in 1890. As a teen-ager, young Aimee was "converted" by her new husband, the American missionary Robert Semple, who took her with him to China. Hardly had the Semples been there when the husband died, leaving Aimee a widow at the age of twenty-one. Mrs. Semple returned to the United States and began a series of Gospel meetings, described by participants as "spectacular." In 1918, Mrs. Semple settled down in Los Angeles and founded the Church of the Four Square Gospel, a soundly fundamentalist organization which preached baptism in the Holy Spirit, speaking in tongues and the power to heal, and the Second Coming of Jesus "in clouds of glory." She also founded a national evangelistic association and a bible college. By 1923, she had completed the one-and-a-half-million-dollar Angelus Temple in Los Angeles.

She married again and became known as Aimee Semple McPherson. Her methods of reaching the masses were a mixture of primitive Pentecostalism and showmanship (for she functioned in the first Golden Age of Hollywood), and much criticism resulted from her flamboyant preachings. But she took credit for feeding 1.5 million poor people. Like a few others who set high standards for the rest of the world, Mrs. McPherson was not free from a fall. In 1926, she disappeared for thirty-seven days; when she reappeared she claimed that she had been kidnapped and tortured, but evidence was shortly produced which proved she had gone off with a male friend to what tabloid newspapers then liked to call a "love nest."

Despite her failings and her flamboyance, she gained a solid following. The Angelus Temple reported ninety thousand members, and after Mrs. McPherson's death in 1944, the work was taken over by her son Robert. Today, without the appeal of the magnetic, striking, and dramatic Mrs. McPherson, it is barely surviving. Other Pentecostal churches and preachers have seized the limelight.

One of the most successful individuals in spreading Pentecostalism is Oral Roberts, who began in 1949 as a preacher in the Pentecostal Holiness Church, which had grown out of the first Fire-Baptized church. The Pentecostal Holiness Church is one of the moderate-size groups, with less than one hundred thousand members. It is closer to Methodism than some of the other bodies; it teaches modified forms of Wesley's doctrines, but believes in an imminent Second Coming and practices divine healing but not to the exclusion of medicine. Baptism in the Spirit is manifested by speaking in tongues, and services are often marked by "joyous demonstrations."

Seven years after his first sermon, Roberts was preaching Pentecostalism over 600 radio stations and was appearing on 167 television "hours." He found a great response among people who were not Pentecostals, particularly the Methodists. His successes led to battles within the Pentecostal Holiness Church, for Roberts resisted pressures to force his following to join the rather strict confines of the organization. Also, his recently built Oral Roberts University at Tulsa, said to have cost thirty million dollars, was independent of the church, and the leadership wanted it. Roberts refused to turn the university into a strictly Pentecostal institution. In 1968, he broke with the Pentecostal Holiness Church to join the United Methodist Church, an organization with a sad history of schism and reunion. It is now formed of several Methodist organizations and the Evangelical United Brethren to compose the largest Methodist church in the nation.

But Roberts still seems to operate within the charisma of early Pentecostalism, and even of the visionaries of the Ranters and Jumpers. As recently as 1980, Roberts could state that he had a mystical experience. On May 25, at 7:00 P.M., he was standing before the foundations of the City of Faith, a very controversial one-hundred-million-dollar medical complex he had begun in Tulsa. Roberts—so he reported to contributors to his center—had a vision of Jesus. As he stood in silent prayer . . .

. . . I felt an overwhelming presence all around me. When I opened my eyes, there He stood, some 900 feet tall, looking at me. His eyes—Oh! His eyes! He stood a full 300 feet taller than the 600-foot-tall City of Faith. There I was, face to face with Jesus Christ, the Son of the Living God.

Roberts reported that Jesus had told him that He would speak to the partners (the contributors) and "through them, I would build it." Tulsa medical authorities are very much against the project, and some have claimed that the vision is a fraud. But one of the evangelist's aides said, "What he said he saw, he saw."

Along with the efforts of Pentecostal preachers to reach the nation, laymen banded together to spread the news of the baptism in the Spirit. One of the most effective organizations to promote Pentecostalism is the Full Gospel Businessmen's Fellowship. The initiator was a California dairyman, Demos Shakarian, who thought that people should seek out the Holy Spirit while remaining members of their own churches. The Fellowship, which was encouraged by Oral Roberts, went from a dozen members to three hundred thousand in twenty years since its founding in 1951, and, it is still growing. How closely its members apply Christian principles to business can be a moot point. One California businessman, who makes folding knives of a type usually banned by most communities, says that God is "the Senior Partner" in his company. "Each knife must reflect the integrity of management, including our Senior Partner."

A most striking aspect of recent Pentecostalism is its success in reaching members of the Roman Catholic Church, which is slow to accept outside innovations. In June 1973, twenty-two thousand new Pentecostals of all churches, but primarily Roman Catholic (including priests and nuns), came together at Notre Dame, Indiana, for three days of testimony to the Third Person of the Trinity. They heard evangelistic sermons, sang and chanted hymns, embraced each other as brothers and sisters in the Lord, testified to miraculous cures through faith, and spoke in tongues. Three days later, Pope Paul VI wondered aloud at a Vatican audience if "certain groups in search of the Holy Spirit are on the right road."

A Catholic psychologist, Father Eugene Kennedy, was more direct in his criticism of the way in which Pentecostalism was reaching the younger generations. He thought it represented the same impulses and emotions "which we see at work in a singles bar or in encounter groups." He thought Pentecostals might be "people who have grown afraid of their emotions . . . people whose feelings have been repressed by the [formal] structure of the church . . . now coming together in an ambience that suddenly makes it legitimate for them freely to express those emotions." But some of the Catholic hierarchy were more positive. The bishop of Grand Rapids said that Pentecostalism "has shown people that a deeper spiritual life is available to everyone, not just people in monasteries." The bishop of Oklahoma City said about Pentecostalism that "if it is practiced correctly, it doesn't really differ that much from traditional Catholicism." The Catholic sociologist Andrew M. Greeley summed up the issue so far as Catholics are concerned by saying that it appeals primarily to Catholics who lead "very restrictive emotional lives." In Pentecostalism "they have found a way of experiencing controlled ecstasy."

Pentecostalism has many critics, from skeptics and scoffers and lampoonists to serious analysts from such bodies as the Lutheran Church Missouri Synod, a major evangelical church, which contends that Pentecostalism exalts personal experience over the authority of the Bible and that it downgrades the role of Jesus in the process of salvation. Other important mainline churches also condemn the movement, saying it contains elements of "narcissism" and it is sometimes "inward and narrow," and its intense emotionalism produces cults centered around strong-willed personalities.

In reply to criticisms offered by mainline churches, the pastor of the Love Church, a born-again nondenominational body in Centereach, Long Island, says, "We offer people an experience, not a religion." Such churches are increasing rapidly in growth. The pastor of the similar Living Water Christian Outreach Church, in Jamesport, a few miles away, says his congregation will grow from two hundred to one thousand in the space of two years. Of established religion he says, "People are discouraged, bored and tired. Born-again Christians are people trying to reach God." A neighbor, the pastor of one of forty-seven Church of God Assemblies on Long Island, which are also enjoying rapid growth, criticizes the unstructured organization of groups like the Love Church. "They are cropping up like living flowers but they will burn away because they have no governments." A nearby Congregational minister believes that worsening economic conditions bring people into the Pentecostal churches. The pastor of the Love Church replies that the answer is otherwise—that people in his church and similar churches have "received the gift of the Holy Spirit and experienced a change in their lives that makes it possible to communicate with a God that is very real to them."

One of the most striking manifestations of Pentecostalism, or charismatic Christianity—whatever name one wants to use—is found among people under thirty. Their names are countless—Jesus People, Jesus Freaks, Jesus Trippers, Street Christians, the Jesus Way, the Children of God, and many others. There are many common themes, not only an interest in ecology, health foods, and Jesus. But they also share a conviction, all too easily imagined and documented by the media, that mankind is living in its last days. Many have a preference for communal living and a bias against institutional Christianity, though such movements as the Intervarsity Christian Fellowship and the Campus Crusade have been able to enlist thousands of more moderate believers.

A substantial number of the Jesus people have been through the drug scene (they are likely to put their Pentecostalism in drug terms—"the Jesus trip," "the Jesus high," and "high on Jesus"). One tripper said:

Acid trips in the seventh grade, sex in the eighth, the Vietnam War a daily serial on TV since you were nine, parents and school worse than "irrelevant"—meaningless—no wonder that Jesus is making a great comeback.

The Jesus trip is not always an easy path to follow. One of the earliest of the young people's Pentecostal groups, the Children of God, which began in the San Francisco Bay area, was the first to be attacked by a deprogrammer, the famous Ted Patrick. Conditions became so unpleasant for many of the Children that the founder, David Brandt Berg, now in his sixties, moved overseas. Today about 90 percent of the members are believed to be abroad. The sect has had troubles with the law, and, in 1974, the New York Attorney General charged it with "fiscal chicanery, obstruction of justice, mental and physical abuse [of members] including rape." The charges were dropped because the sect was considered to be under the protection of the First Amendment; members said the allegations came from "false witnesses." Berg changed the name of the sect to the Family of Love. Controversy continues to follow the group no matter what the name. In 1979, the *New York Times* reported that Berg "extols women members to be 'fishers of men,' " that is, to seduce men who might be potential converts or possible wealthy backers. The practice is known as "flirty-fishing," and is actually a form of prostitution on behalf of the sect, for the women must turn over whatever money, jewels, and other gifts they receive.

It is clear that religion in America, as elsewhere, takes strange and often dramatic forms. Even some of the long-established Holiness and Pentecostal churches engage in unusual practices evolved from their special interpretation of the Holy Scriptures. These practices have brought them criticism, and would result in deprogramming and criminal prosecution if they were engaged in by young people. The so-called reptile handlers, who belong within the general framework of the Church of God congregations, give an extreme example of their baptism in the Holy Spirit not only by speaking in tongues and practicing divine healing, but by taking up serpents and drinking deadly liquids.

THE CHURCHES OF GOD

Summer 1909, rural Grasshopper Valley, Tennessee. George Went Hensley, a fundamentalist pastor in his early thirties, pondered Mark 16:17, 18, got a rattlesnake, and began to "handle" it at services. Mark 16:17, 18 reads:

> And these signs shall follow them that believe; In my name shall they cast out devils; they shall speak with new tongues;
> They shall take up serpents; and if they drink any deadly thing, it shall not hurt them; they shall lay hands on the sick, and they shall recover.

Thus Hensley had found a biblical guarantee that the handling of serpents would not bring harm. Later he went over to the East Pineville Church of God at Pine Mountain, about seven miles from Harlan, Kentucky, and there, too, he employed snakes in worship.

The snakes were not harmless grass snakes or green snakes but rattlesnakes, not defanged or milked as skeptics eventually charged, but very much alive and poisonous—ornery and fatal when aroused. In handling snakes, Hensley was not testing his faith but showing proof that Jesus really did say that if people "shall take up serpents . . . it shall not hurt them."

Soon other church members took up snakes. No one was forced to handle them. It was purely a question of personal choice, based entirely on the conviction that at the moment the handler was filled with the Holy Spirit.

The Holy Spirit is very much a part of the lives of the people in the remote area of the Appalachian chain of mountains. Many of them are members of one of the fundamentalist Holiness churches congregated under the broad title of "Church of God," or some other variation of that name. The Church of God people in the Pineville area and the neighboring hamlets and towns believe, along with other Holiness and Pentecostal members, that the Holy Spirit confers supernatural gifts—the ability to speak in tongues, to heal by prayer, and to cast out demons. They also practice the laying on of hands and anointing by oil.

Most of the churches forbid worldly practices such as theater-going, dancing, smoking, drinking, immodest dress, and the cutting of women's hair. Some members will still not drink that southern staple, cola drinks. Church members call each other "saint" by way of greeting, and often the men kiss each other.

Hensley thought he was the first person to take up snakes. He did so spontaneously, but there are obscure references that the practice was known in at least two other places about the time Hensley handled his first reptile. There is some evidence that A. J. Tomlinson, the progenitor of a series of Holiness and Pentecostal bodies, handled poisonous snakes in the hamlet of Cherokee, North Carolina, in 1903, about the time he joined the Church of God. Snake handling as part of a Christian religious service has also been traced back as early as 1906 in Los Angeles, according to Weston La Barre, an anthropologist. Whether or not the three isolated and different instances have some connection with each other cannot be determined, says La Barre.

Upon Hensley's death, the practice of snake handling appeared to die out. However, a disciple of Hensley's, a man named Raymond Hayes, kept up snake handling for almost forty years. In 1943, he established a church at Grasshopper Valley, where Hensley had first practiced. The new church was called the Dolley Pond Church of God with Signs Following, named after Mark 16:1–7 ("and these signs shall follow them"). Dolley Pond became the mother church of the snake handlers.

The practice of handling snakes might have languished in obscurity for centuries, but two Church of God ministers were bitten and died in 1945. The Associated Press sent the story out on national wire, and the Dolley Pond church gained national publicity, with stories in *Look*, then a biweekly picture magazine, and other leading publications and newspapers. Some of the articles were fairly accurate; others were wildly speculative to the point of hysteria. After further deaths from snakebite, the practice of handling snakes was banned in Tennessee but spread to other states. About this time the practice of drinking strychnine cocktails was adopted, with a few resulting deaths. Snake handling and related practices were now firmly established as a national curiosity. The churches did not mind the publicity, for they saw it as a means of bringing in the unfaithful, the unchurched, and the sinners to the worship of the true Lord God.

From the outset there were many misconceptions. The handling of snakes was widely reported—and still is—as a "test of faith," or as a test of "the proof of godliness." However, the one and only purpose is to "confirm the faith"—that is, it is not a test but a confirmation of Jesus' words: "They shall take up serpents; and if they drink any deadly thing, it shall not hurt them." This passage is Christ's guarantee that no harm will come to the practitioner. Thus, to handle snakes or to drink deadly things without harm is to confirm the very truth of His word. The handling of snakes by the faithful is proof of God's love and protection, of His power and His strength. One of the churches obtained an Indian cobra, an extremely deadly serpent, and some of the members would put it inside their shirts and let it move about. Two young researchers, Karen W. Carden and Robert W. Pelton, who interviewed many of the snake handlers (for their rather uncritical work, *The Persecuted Prophets*), report the Reverend Floyd McCall as saying:

I got a different anointing to handle the cobra. I got anointed from head to toe. I felt like I was walking on the world. I'd never felt anything like it before. That feeling stayed on me the whole time the cobra was in my hands. This was the most powerful I'd ever been anointed to take up a serpent. I couldn't sit still. I was jumping up and down, running around—I felt as light as a feather. It was a strange feeling in my bones.

"Anoint" is the common description of the power given by the Lord to the men and women who not only handle serpents but drink deadly liquids, engage in healing practices, sometimes practice exorcism, and take up fire.

Sometimes the anointing seems to fail at a crucial moment, and the brother or sister is bitten by a snake, or dies of a deadly drink. There are two reasons for the failure. Being bitten "in the will of God" may be a sign to the unbeliever of the credibility of the snake handler, for there are those who inaccurately accuse church members of defanging or milking the snakes. A deadly, fatal bite proves to scoffers and sceptics that indeed this is a very poisonous reptile that is handled. A second reason for being bitten is that God uses the serpent to discipline a beloved transgressor. "Unable as humans are to remain sinless, these Christians expect punishment from their Master. The bite is a reminder to obey," say Carden and Pelton.

When a member dies of snakebite, the congregation can equate it with the suffering of Jesus. On April 2, 1974, about 8:30 P.M., Richard Lee Williams of Hilliard, Ohio, while conducting a revival service at the Full Gospel Jesus Church in Kustley, West Virginia, was bitten by a diamondback rattler. He had handled it safely once, returned it to its box, and then picked it up later. The rattler struck him in the palm of the hand. Williams dropped the snake back into its box, but then apparently decided that he should continue with the handling. When he reached for the snake again, it sank its fangs into an artery in his wrist. Williams spoke reassuringly to the congregation, after which he went to the nearby home of a member. His arm soon swelled to a grotesque size. He died around three o'clock the next afternoon, aged thirty-three— "Like Jesus," pointed out members of the congregation of the Full Gospel Jesus Church.

Floyd McCall was noted for drinking Drano as well, and Brother Buford Pack had taken battery acid. But, as in the case of handling serpents, there seemed to be an inevitable time when the test of faith failed. The crisis came for the Reverend Jimmy Williams, a preacher, and Pack when they took strychnine at the Holiness Church of God in Jesus at Newport, Tennessee, on April 8, 1973. The two died. Pack's brother, Liston Pack, was the pastor of the church and since the deaths had occurred theoretically under his responsibility, local officials, understandably disturbed, ordered an investigation. A month after the tragedy, a grand jury ruled for a verdict of suicide, thus clearing Liston Pack of the charge of involuntary manslaughter.

Though Mark 16 does not mention fire, the Holiness churches include it in their practices, for there is biblical sanction for its use as proof of the Lord's love. The second half of Isaiah 43:2 reads:

When thou walkest through the fire, thou shalt not be burned; neither shall the flame kindle upon thee.

Then there is the story in Daniel of Shadrach, Meshach, and Abednego, who were cast into a fiery furnace by Nebuchadnezzar for their refusal to worship the golden image. The flames did not harm them. The king said to his courtiers:

Lo, I see four men loose, walking in the midst of the fire, and they have no hurt; and the form of the fourth is like the Son of God.
[When they came out of the flames, it was seen that] these men upon whose bodies the fire had no power, nor was a hair of their head singed, neither were their coats changed, nor the smell of fire had passed on them.

The Saints use blow torches, or torches made of soft drink bottles filled with kerosene, with cotton wads in the neck as a wick. The torch is passed around the church, and those of the Saints who have the anointing, men and women, fan their hands and arms through the flames. Some of the faithful might speak in tongues, or sing hymns as they handle it. Fire is a less dangerous proof of the Lord's love than rattlers or strychnine, and it can puzzle even the most skeptical outsider. A psychiatrist, Dr. Berthold E. Schwartz, stated with some amazement that "I have seen thirteen members of the Holiness sect, men and women, handle fire, and of these I could say the same: upon their bodies the fire had no power."

The flames are orange-yellow and shoot eight inches to two feet high. The worshipers slowly move their outstretched open hands and fingers over the midpoint of the flames for times ranging from three to five seconds or even longer. On three occasions, two of the "Saints" put their exposed toes and the soles of their feet directly into the flames for five to fifteen seconds.

Schwartz mentions a man who turned to a coal fire burning for an hour, picked up a flaming coal the size of an egg, and "held it in the palms of his hands for sixty-five seconds while he walked among the congregation." Schwartz says he found that "I could not touch a piece of burning charcoal for a fraction of a second without developing a painful blister."

It is these extreme forms of establishing His powers that set Holiness churches apart. But in other practices and beliefs, they run parallel to many other fundamentalist and even traditional bodies. Like many churches, they are millennialists and expect the imminent Second Coming of the Lord, the end of the world, and the Last Judgment. For the Saints there is but one book, the Bible, and they know it with a thoroughness that is otherworldly to the outsider.

In theology, many members depart radically from older, traditional churches, and even from other born-in-America sects. Saints like Brother Jimmy Ray Williams put the emphasis on Jesus alone as Lord and God, and not on the Trinity in the classical sense.

The name of Jesus Christ has caused the worst confusion of anything. And we believe only in him. The Father, the Son, and the Holy Ghost, are only names for Jesus Christ. We don't baptize people in Their Name but in the name of Jesus Christ alone.

That Name bears tremendous powers, one of which is expressed in the common practice of healing. Sister Bea had given testimony of what has happened to her. Sometime in the 1960s she suffered "a blood problem." She went to Brother Rubie Campbell at Sand Hill Church for help.

Brother Campbell had laid his hands on me as he prayed. I could feel the strength coming back into my weakened body. I've not had any trouble with this since.

However, some five years later she ran into other trouble.

I had something wrong with my left eye. There was a growth or something behind it that caused a lot of pain. The doctor, after an eye examination, said I was nearly blind in the left eye, and I needed to wear special glasses all the time. I wasn't supposed to ever take those glasses off.

Carden and Pelton reported what happened when Sister Bea returned to Brother Campbell. When he prayed and laid hands on her, "the pain stopped and her vision immediately returned to normal. She can see today [1974] as well out of her left eye as her right, and the pain has not returned."

One more example of widespread and successful healing will suffice. Sister Eunice, eighteen, had been suffering a constant headache, frequent blackouts, and was under the care of a "well-known" (but not named) Tennessee neurologist. He informed her that she had a brain tumor and had to undergo surgery. One night the pastor of the church rose and called upon everyone present to lay hands on Sister Eunice. "I've never felt the anointing like I feel it tonight," said the pastor. The entire congregation came forth to touch her or to touch someone else who was touching her.

It felt like something that just ran from the top of my head to the bottom of my feet. Like a bolt of something hit me. The pain disappeared when "that" hit me. It didn't hurt, it felt good. It was very quick. I didn't have any more trouble with it after this. When I went back to the doctor, he couldn't find any trace of the tumor.

The reptile-handling churches exist primarily in the Appalachian mountain chain, or in the poorer fringes of some of the big southern and midwestern cities. The members are for the most part what sociologists describe as lower middle class; there seem to be no well-off members. Virtually all Saints are whites, of the rugged Anglo-Saxon and Scotch-Irish ancestry that came down from the north seeking new frontiers after New England and New York State dried up as lands of opportunity a century and a half ago. Many of the people work in the great mills—cotton, industrial, tobacco—and are always on the edge of poverty. They lead routinized, monotonous lives in a paternalistic environment which rarely allows them to rise above the level of semiskilled workers. Conditions in the factories and mills are far from ideal, with high humidity, constant noise, heat in the summer, and clattering machines which never stop and keep laborers under unending pressure. Often the worker's wife is also a mill girl, on another shift, holding the job to make ends meet. It is, says Weston La Barre, who has studied the churches, "a life of poverty under a personal God of stern rewards and punishment" with "religious conformity . . . dissenters of all kinds risk hellfire." He adds: "Goaded by godly as well as by secular standards, the mill worker is puritanical, fanatic, narrow-minded and fundamentalist." In general, the churches, as with many southern Methodist, Baptist, and Presbyterian churches, frown on smoking, drinking, divorce, and unsanctioned sexuality. Hellfire threatens as often as heaven beckons. God's punishing hand is as common as His saving Hand.

Still there are joy and ecstacy in the lives of the Saints. Though secular dancing is considered sinful, music and dancing in the churches are standard, and with an exuberance that astounds the spectator. The services are relatively unstructured, with none of the formalities of the older churches, of the balletlike liturgy of a Roman Catholic or Anglican high mass, of the communion services of the Presbyterians and Methodists. All is spontaneous, improvised along certain accepted patterns, a free outpouring of the soul and psyche to the Lord. People sit in silence, or break out in song and shouts of praise and of joy as the Spirit demands. Like the frontier congregations of the 1800s, to which the Church of God people are heirs, members may reach such peaks of spiritual intensity that they may "fall like soldiers," fainting with the exuberance of the enveloping Spirit. It is an intensely private experience, yet every member wants to share it with the others.

Schwartz has described a typical meeting. After introductory hymns accompanied by guitars, cymbals, and tambourines, and prayers said aloud, various members testify and confess sins and offer repentance. Experiences are related to passages in the Bible. Fervor increases as "the power of the Lord" quickens in the faithful and exhaltation becomes widespread.

Now they are shouting, screaming, crying, singing, jerking, jump-

ing, twitching, whistling, hooting, gesturing, swaying, swooning, trembling, strutting, goosestepping, stamping; and incoherently [to Schwartz] they "speak in new tongues."

All of this, from the initial singing and the testimonies to the states of exhaltation, sounds like the Jumpers witnessed by John Wesley, as well as other sects, including the Shakers. When the excitement and fervor in the church has climaxed, those of the Saints who wish to take up reptiles or drink deadly drinks or handle flames do so.

Though the handling of snakes, the drinking of deadly poisons, or the taking up of fire is a purely personal decision, the law, in whatever form—local, state, and even federal—takes a harsh view of the Saints and their practices. Many of the Saints have been arrested and imprisoned for their beliefs. Laws have been passed by localities and states against the handling of snakes. In virtually all cases they have been challenged by the churches, sometimes with the aid of civil rights legal organizations. During confrontations with the law, including arrests and trials, the Saints never become resentful, angry, or bitter. The general comment is that their faith is being tried for the good of the Gospel. "We'd all be willing to go to jail," says Sister Thelma Whittaker. "Yes, I'd violate the law, because I'm obeying God's Word which is more important. . . . If it's in the Scripture, then we do whatever He tells us we must do."

The communal feeling is deep. Willie Sizemore says, "I fast for other people and the church," an act not likely to be found in older denominations. Sizemore also says, "I expect great spiritual benefits and more spiritual power from it. I believe fasting takes you a whole lot closer to God. It makes you more spiritual." This closeness to God is a feeling that most of the Saints share. "You've never been on a trip until you feel the Holy Ghost in you," remarks Brother Ralph Eslinger, meaning that the experience of God is more powerful than that of drugs. "There's one thing about it, you won't wake up with a headache, a hangover, or in a jail cell. It's the happiest trip you can be on—the anointing of the Holy Ghost."

7

AMERICAN INDIAN
RELIGIONS

A T THE END OF THE EIGHTEENTH CENTURY, AN AGING
Seneca Indian named Handsome Lake (Ca-ne-o-di-yo in his
own tongue) experienced a series of visions which radically
changed his life. Handsome Lake was a ranking sachem, a tribal
leader, by birth a Seneca of the Turtle Clan. He was a half brother
of the famous Cornplanter, who had been instrumental in organizing the five Indian nations of what is now New York State into
the federation known as the Iroquois League.

For most of his sixty-four years, Handsome Lake had led a
dissolute life. Around 1799, after four years of illness, he lay dying

in a small village in northern Pennsylvania, with no hope of recovery and resigned to death. He had fallen into insensibility, and his brothers Cornplanter and Blacksnake believed he had already passed away, though portions of his body were still warm. At noon he revived and spoke to his family, telling them of the vision he had just experienced. In what were apparently his last moments, three spiritual beings came to him in the forms of men, sent by the Great Spirit. Each messenger bore in his hand a different miraculous shrub, each with berries, which Handsome Lake ate, as directed by his visitors. He was immediately restored to health. The trio then spoke to him of the will of the Great Spirit on many subjects and instructed him to pass on the doctrines to the Iroquois. Then he was shown the "realm of the Evil-Minded" where he saw the punishments afflicted upon the wicked, after which the heavenly home of the virtuous was revealed to him. (As in the case of other prophets and visionaries among both Indians and whites, the accounts of what happened and what the true message was have come down in different versions, and putting them together sometimes leads to discrepancies.)

In further visions a fourth divine messenger joined the original three, giving Handsome Lake what was to become known as the Good Message. The Message, or "Code," as it is sometimes called, resembled that given to other Indian prophets of other tribes, from the Atlantic to the Pacific. The Great Spirit had made man—the Indian, not the white—"pure and good." The Great Spirit did not intend that man should sin, but man sinned, the common cause being "fire water"—hard liquor.

Today the Good Message is repeated periodically in the longhouses—the sacred temples—of the Iroquois nations, and it runs in part like this:

You commit a great sin in taking the fire-water. The Great Spirit says that you must abandon this enticing habit. Your ancestors have brought great misery and suffering upon you. They first took the fire-water of the white man, and entailed upon you its consequences. None of them have gone to heaven. The fire-water does not belong to you. It was made for the white man beyond the waters. For the white man it is a medicine; but they too have violated the will of their Maker.

The theme of drunkenness was taken up again in the Message. But equally important was the question of the earth, one which other Indian prophets, seers, visionaries, leaders, and chiefs were to stress. The land is sacred and inviolate. The Indians hold it in common, not individually as whites do.

The Great Spirit, when He made the earth, never intended that it should be made merchandise; but He willed that all His creatures should enjoy it equally. Your chiefs have violated and betrayed your trust by selling lands. Nothing is now left of our once large possessions, save a few small reservations. . . . Whoever sells lands offends the Great Spirit, and must expect a great punishment after death.

Land, stressed Handsome Lake, is a sacred trust held for one's children.

A major point in the Code was that of rejecting white customs and influences. Though it allowed Indians to raise cattle and build warm and comfortable houses (the Iroquois lived in bark houses, not tepees), these were "all they could safely adopt of the customs of the palefaces. You cannot live as they do."

There are Christian influences in the Message, with echoes of the Sermon on the Mount. No one who repented could be damned, even if repentance came at the end of a sinful life. Poverty was not sinful, as the Congregationalists might have preached at the time in their Calvinistic doctrine of the good being rewarded with earthly wealth while the wicked languished in privation. "It is better to be poor on earth and rich in the sky-world [heaven] than to have earth riches and no heaven."

Christ was seen as the Indians saw Him everywhere, as One murdered by the whites—not the Indians. Thus the red men had no responsibility for the crimes against Jesus. In one of his visions Handsome Lake met a man whose hands and feet and breast were wounded and smeared with fresh blood.

They slew me [says the man to Handsome Lake] because of their independence and unbelief. So I have gone home to shut the doors of Heaven that they may not see me again until the earth passes away.

The Man asked the prophet how the Iroquois received his teachings. Handsome Lake replied that "about half my people are inclined to believe in me." The Man said:

You are more successful than I, for some believe in you but none in me. I am inclined to believe in the end it will also be so with you. Now, it is rumored that you are but a talker with spirits. Now, it is true that I am a spirit and the one of Him who was murdered. Now, tell your people that they will become lost when they follow the ways of the white man.

The Quakers had been active in the area, and some of their influences were noted in the Code. They preached an uncompromising pacifism, and Handsome Lake picked up this doctrine and was credited with keeping the Senecas from taking up arms for the British against the Americans in the War of 1812.

Handsome Lake's teachings spread outside the Iroquois League. Thomas Jefferson, then president of the United States, heard of him and invited the prophet to the White House with a delegation of sachems. The President was deeply impressed and gave Handsome Lake a letter in which he urged the Indians to follow the Good Message. This letter was included in the sacred documents of the longhouse churches.

How one views a prophet depends by and large on one's own culture. To the Iroquois, Handsome Lake—with his doctrines of the preservation of Indian customs, traditions, rights, family, and attitudes (especially of the sacredness of the earth)—is a savior and messiah. But whites in most instances saw and still see him as a threat. A white writer, Thomas R. Henry, writing as recently as 1955, called him "extremely reactionary," for Handsome Lake "opposed missions, schools, white methods of agriculture, and above all, 'business.' " Handsome Lake had allowed that the Indians "might farm a little and build houses, but they must not sell anything they raised but give it away to another." A most "Christian" attitude, but one which implied a threat to white values.

The Code of Handsome Lake spread throughout the Iroquois League, though in the face of fierce opposition from Catholic and Protestant missionaries. Today an estimated third of the members of the Iroquois Nations are members of the Handsome Lake longhouses, and its appeal is growing in part due to the new sense of nationalism and identity among the Iroquois, as among all Indians. There are major meetings three times a year in the longhouses, as well as others, attended not only by the faithful but also by the Christians, who may stand or crouch outside in the grass to hear the Message. Preachers go from village to village to repeat the Code to the people. Because the tribes speak different though related languages, there are many variations in the exact wording of the Message, which was for a long time passed down orally. Also, the languages have changed over the years and some words and terms are now archaic and not always clear. The broad theme for the Iroquois peoples is one of reformation, salvation, and hope, with a rejection of the ways of the white man, his customs, and practices, especially of the notorious fire water.

Handsome Lake is buried at the Onandaga reservation, a few miles south of Syracuse, New York. In 1815, he had been living quietly at Tonawanda in the western part of the state, near Niagara Falls. He was invited to visit Onandaga, and on the way he had a vision which showed him a pathway of grass leading to the New World, that is, heaven. On arriving at Onandaga the prophet fell ill and died. His body lies opposite the Onandaga longhouse.

About the same time that Handsome Lake was preaching in New York State, a Shawnee, Tenskwatawa, experienced visions that told him that his people should relinquish white ways and return to traditional Indian customs. This would give the Shawnees the strength to resist the whites. The prophet's brother, Tecumseh, enlivened by the success of Tenskwatawa's prophecies among the Indians, rallied his people against the oncoming strangers in the hope of halting their advance into Shawnee lands.

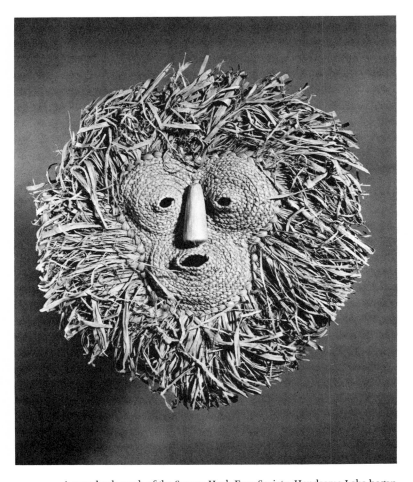

A corn husk mask of the Seneca Husk Face Society. Handsome Lake began his preaching in the lodges of the various men's societies of the Iroquois League. The ceremonies dealing with corn, a basic and sacred food, remained important in the Good Message. PHOTOGRAPH COURTESY OF MUSEUM OF THE AMERICAN INDIAN, HEYE FOUNDATION

The Great Spirit gave this great island [America] to his red children [said Tecumseh]. He placed the white man on the other side of the big water. They were not content with their own land but came to take ours from us. They have driven us from the sea to the lakes, we can go no further.

In battles in 1811 and 1812 the Indians were defeated, and with Tenskwatawa discredited, the movement died out. A few years later the Kickapoos in Illinois were told by their prophet Kanakuk that if they led honest lives and followed the religious rites he had devised, they would not be driven from their lands by the whites. A period of intense religiosity followed in the expectation of salvation and long life for the tribe. But the whites advanced anyway, in 1852, driving the Kickapoos out of their lands. They took refuge in Kansas, where Kanakuk came down with smallpox and died. His people had believed that should he ever die, he would arise in three days. While sitting with the body in expectation of its resurrection, many of the Kickapoos also contracted smallpox, and the disease wiped out the tribe.

Prophets appeared everywhere, seeing the Great Spirit in visions, and in the course of the sun and the moon, and the stars. They brought back the message of hope to their people, so hardset in their struggle against the white tide that was engulfing them and their lands and destroying their lives and their sacred customs. One of the most important of the nineteenth-century prophets was Smoholla or Smoqual, the "Preacher," a Wanapum living on the confluence of the Columbia and Snake rivers, near the Washington-Oregon border. Smoholla was also called Shouting Mountain, for part of his revelation had come from a mountain which had spoken to him as he lay asleep on the summit. He was known as a healer and shaman. A major turn in his career came after he was left for dead in a duel with another shaman, named Moses. His body was thrown on the banks of a river. The waters carried him away, but he was rescued by a white settler. Instead of returning to his village, Smoholla journeyed as far south as Mexico before coming home with the message to his people that the Great Spirit wanted them to give up white ways and to go back to their own customs. His trances and visions were constant, and so he was also known as the Dreamer. In his visions he learned that the Indians were the first people; only the Indians were of the stock created by God. From the Indians came the others, the whites and the negroes. Thus it followed that the earth belonged to the Indians.

You asked me to plow the ground [Smoholla said to his people].
Shall I take a knife and tear my mother's bosom? Then when I die
she will not take me into her bosom to rest. . . . You ask me to cut
grass and make hay and sell it and be rich like white men! But
how dare I cut my mother's hair!

Smoholla introduced several dances, the most notable of which was the Dream Dance, which often sent the participants into trances during which they experienced visions they later recounted in public. Among the Indians influenced by the Dreamer were the Nez Percés in the nearby Wallowa Valley of Oregon. After the federal government had broken contracts guaranteeing the tribe's ancestral lands, troops under General Howard tried to force the Nez Percés to move to a reservation in the spring of 1877. The land no longer belonged to the Indians, as God had assured the Dreamer it did. The Nez Percés, led by Chief Joseph, tried to escape the army. Howard pursued them over a wandering route, some twelve hundreds miles of rugged and dangerous country, with constant running battles. Joseph brought his people to Montana, a few miles from the border of Canada, where he hoped to take refuge. But a second force of soldiers had meanwhile come from the east, cutting off the Nez Percés, and they had to surrender. Joseph's speech to General Howard was widely published at the time, and remains a classic statement of the tragedy of the American Indian, ill-equipped, trusting, and betrayed in the face of the might of a modern industrial society, ruthless and amoral in its aims. Joseph said, in summary:

I am tired of fighting. Our chiefs are killed, Looking Glass is dead.
The old men are all dead. It is the young men who say yes or no.
It is cold and we have no blankets. The little children are freezing

to death. No food. I want to have time to look for my children and see how many I can find. Maybe I shall find them among the dead. Hear me, my chiefs, I am tired; my heart is sick and sad. From where the sun now stands I will fight no more forever.

The government had promised that the Nez Percés would be allowed to settle on a reservation in Oregon, but again the white man broke his contract. The tribe was shipped off to Oklahoma, to the so-called Indian Territory. Smoholla's Dream Dance had brought only sorrow to the Indians. The white man owned the land.

Still, prophecy was not dead, despite the tragic conclusions to the dreams and hopes entertained by every tribe that followed a prophet. Another prophet would arise, and then another, and another, until the American Indian finally lay crushed by his own faith. Of all the victims, the Sioux are among the most heroic and the most tragic.

THE GHOST DANCE

Who would have thought that dancing could make such trouble? We had no wish to make trouble, nor did we cause it of ourselves. There was trouble, but it was not of my making. We had no thought of fighting; if we had meant to fight, would we not have carried arms? We went unarmed to the dance. How could we have held weapons? For thus we danced, in a circle, hand in hand, each man's fingers linked with those of his neighbor.

Who would have thought that dancing could make such trouble? For the message that I brought was peace. And the message was given by the Father to all the tribes.

The words belong to Short Bull—Tatanka-Ptecila in his own tongue—a Sioux medicine man from the Rosebud Indian Reservation in South Dakota, speaking to his people about the Ghost Dance of the Plains Indians of 1879 and 1880, an event which seriously alarmed whites and brought an end to Indian hopes of freedom.

Short Bull, one of the most prominent of the Ghost Dance leaders, was revered among his people as a great medicine man, a prophet, and a worker of miracles. The Sioux (also known as the Dakota and the Lakota—meaning "many in one") honored him as one of the pilgrims who had sought out the Father, a Nevada Paiute prophet known as Wovoka. Wovoka preached a message of hope and salvation. He said the Indians, all Indians, would soon be free of white domination if they would but follow his teachings. His doctrines centered around a new sacred dance, in which the participants would often fall "dead," that is, go into a trance, in which they would ascend to heaven and see again their hallowed dead, their ancestors and friends, and the children who had prematurely passed away. Soon, too, the world would be renewed, the herds would return, the grass would grow lush and green again, and the whites would disappear.

Short Bull, in company with ten other Sioux, had visited Wovoka in the summer of 1890, traveling to Nevada by the newly completed transcontinental railroad. In Nevada they were greeted by two strange Indians, obviously expecting them, who gave them food and horses and took them to an encampment of Paiutes near Pyramid Lake, in the western part of the state. Here the Paiutes told them that Christ had returned to earth again, and that He must have sent for the Sioux. Another journey, through mountainous territory, brought them to Walker Lake, the home of the Messiah. Here the Sioux, along with hundreds of Indians from dozens of tribes, waited for two days. On the evening of the third day the Messiah appeared, and a huge fire was built to enable the Indians to see Him. Short Bull's brother-in-law, Kicking Bear, remarked later that he thought Jesus was a white man, but this one looked like an Indian. After a while the Messiah arose and spoke. Short Bull reported his words.

Behold, I tell you something for you to tell all the people! Give this dance to all the different tribes of Indians. White people and Indians shall all dance together. But first they shall sing. There shall be no more fighting. No man shall kill another. If any man should be killed, it would be a grievous thing. No man shall lie. Love one an-

other. Help one another. Do not revile one another. Hear me, for I will give you water to drink. Thus I tell you, this is why I have called you. My meaning—have you understood it?

Wovoka was about thirty-three at the time of Short Bull's visit. The facts and the details surrounding him are far from clear, for they have been reported by Indians who did not speak his language, or by whites, many of whom were hostile. Even Wovoka's own statements about his visions do not always dovetail, possibly because in conversations he emphasized whatever seemed to be important at the moment. The most accurate and the best information comes from James Mooney, a young ethnologist, who gathered together various reports about Wovoka, took part in Ghost Dances himself, was at the Rosebud reservation at the time of the Ghost Dance movement among the Sioux, and finally visited Wovoka. Mooney's work, entitled *The Ghost-Dance Religion and the Sioux Outbreak of 1890*, is the book upon which all others are based in whole or in part.

In studying the various reports, Mooney's as well as other sources, the following seems like a reasonable account of Wovoka's career and the excitement that ensued. It was and is a custom in many Indian tribes for the young males at puberty, or shortly afterward, to go into isolation, either alone or with two or three companions of the same age. They do this in order to enter into the mystical visions that lead into manhood and give them a place among the ranks of the braves. Not all men are fortunate enough to receive the sacred visions. What Wovoka experienced went beyond the ordinary, and set him apart from others. It must also be said that it is difficult to establish whether the events in his visionary experience were literal or symbolic.

About the age of fourteen, Wovoka received a great revelation, falling asleep in the daytime—it seems to have been during an eclipse of the sun—and was taken up into the other world. Here he saw God, with all the people who had died long ago, forever young, enjoying their former sports and games and occupations— all this in a land full of wild animals. God, said Wovoka, then told him he must go back to his own people and tell them they must be good and love one another, not quarrel, and live in peace with the whites. They must work and not lie or steal, they must not engage in war, and if they faithfully obeyed the Lord's instructions they would be reunited with those in the other world, where there would no longer be death or sickness or old age. God then gave the young man the dance which he was commanded to pass on to his people. The dance was to be performed over a period of five days. Finally, God gave Wovoka control over the elements so that he could make it rain or snow or be dry at will. Wovoka returned to earth and preached as he had been instructed. However, as Mooney reported it, Wovoka did not instruct his people in the new dance for another two years.

There is much confusion here, for Mooney added a statement by another Paiute who placed the events some fifteen years later, when Wovoka was roughly thirty. He may have been confused with another prophet, Tavibo, who was sometimes described as his father, sometimes as his spiritual master. Tavibo was prophesizing about 1870, when Wovoka was fourteen, and the events in the life of one seer could easily have merged with those of the other. Both men were members of a long line of such prophets among the Paiutes, a tribe of some eight thousand people spread throughout Nevada, Utah, and the neighboring areas. Tavibo ("White Man"—but he was definitely an Indian) had announced a series of revelations around 1870. He had gone, alone, up the mountain, and there met the Great Spirit, who gave him a message of hope and redemption for the Indians, for everywhere the whites had taken their lands and hunting grounds and destroyed their ancestral ways. The Paiutes had been reduced almost to the level of peonage and destitution. In his repeated visions, Tavibo was told that the land would be returned to the Indians; the whites would be swallowed up in a great earthquake, while the Indians would be "saved and permitted to enjoy the earth and the fullness thereof, including anything left by the wicked whites." Also, the Indians would "live forever to enjoy the earth, with plenty of game, fish, and pine nuts." Among those to hear the prophet were believers and skeptics. However, Tavibo's message traveled afar, and the Indians of other tribes from Idaho and Oregon came to investigate.

A final vision stated that only those Indians who believed would be saved; the others would be damned together with the whites.

But in the twenty years between Tavibo's visions in 1870 and Wovoka's preaching in 1889 and 1890, there were other happenings. There were stories of other prophets, "two mysterious beings with white skins," who announced, "a speedy resurrection of all the dead Indians, the restoration of game, and a return of the oldtime primitive life. Under the new order of things both races alike [are] to be white." This was around 1875, and the Indians, not only the Paiutes but other tribes as well, were quite excited. There was also talk of a new ceremonial dance being performed at night in a circle, without the traditional fire of other dances.

Whatever the dates of Wovoka's visions, the new dance was firmly established in Nevada, being practiced by both Indians and whites, when pilgrims from faraway tribes began to seek out the Messiah. One of the groups was led by a warrior named Porcupine, a Cheyenne from Montana, who had been working his way from one tribe to another. He finally met a group of Bannocks, who led him at last, one night, into the presence of a man everyone called "Christ."

Porcupine later gave a detailed statement to a Major Carroll in command of the reservation at Tongue River, Montana, which is condensed here.

Just after dark some of the Indians told me that the Christ was arrived. I had always thought the Great Father was a white man, but this man looked like an Indian. He sat there a long time and nobody went up to speak to him. He sat with his head bowed all the time. After a while he rose and said he was very glad to see his children. "I have sent for you and am glad to see you. I am going to talk to you after a while about your relatives who are dead and gone. My children, I want you to listen to all I have to say to you. I will teach you, too, how to dance a dance, and I want you to dance it. Get ready for your dance and then, when the dance is over, I will talk to you." Then he commenced to dance our dance, everybody joining in, the Christ singing while we danced.

Porcupine was curious about the Christ. "I had heard that the Christ had been crucified, and I looked to see, and I saw a scar on his wrist and one on his face, and he seemed to be the man. I could not see his feet."

The next day, after breakfast, the Christ talked to the assembled tribes, who formed a circle around him, sitting on the ground.

He said: "I am the man who made everything you see around you. I am not lying to you, my children. I made this earth and everything on it. I have been to heaven and seen your dead friends and have seen my own father and mother. In the beginning, after God made the earth, they sent me back to teach the people, and when I came back on earth the people were afraid of me and treated me badly. This is what they did to me [showing his scars]. I did not try to defend myself. I found my children were bad, so I went back to heaven and left them. I told them that in so many hundred years I would come back to see my children. At the end of this time I was sent back to try to teach them. My father told me the earth was getting old and worn out, and the people getting bad, and that I was to renew everything as it used to be, and make it better.

The Messiah also told the Indians that the dead would be resurrected, that no one should fight, and that all people, Indians and whites alike, would be friends. The earth would be renewed, and no one would be older than forty years, and that all wounds and sickness would be healed, and that everyone would live forever. Porcupine went home, and began to tell people about the Christ. He even told the whites, remarking to Major Carroll, "I thought all of you people knew all of this I have told you, but it seems you do not."

The word passed from tribe to tribe on both sides of the Rockies—"A Savior has arisen for the Indian people." Delegates from everywhere visited Wovoka and returned convinced that a new day was about to dawn for the Indian. His teachings began to develop in the telling as they were carried back to the home reservations. For many the prophet was indeed Jesus come again to earth—Jesus, who long ago had come beyond the waters to the whites, who killed Him, was now returned to the Indians, "who never did Him harm." Wovoka explicitly told Mooney that he never made a claim to being Christ, nor was he divine in any way, yet the belief persisted. Mooney decided that Wovoka might have languished in obscurity if it were not for the fact of the encroaching modern world. The new Union Pacific Railroad had made it easy for Indians to visit the prophet. Young Indians forced into the government boarding schools wrote each other and their relatives on the reservations about Wovoka. They acted as interpreters to the delegates visiting the Messiah, and in various ways assumed the leadership of the Ghost Dance.

By the time the news reached the Plains Indians, it had been somewhat changed. Not only would the spirits of the dead return, the old days come back, and the buffalo flourish as they did in the time before the white man came to deplete the herds, but the whites would be swept back across the sea in a mighty cataclysm. In some versions they would be overcome with a wave of mud and buried. Wovoka's message of both races living in harmony was gone. Some of the Sioux believed that they were to go to the mountains to escape, while the whites perished. Others thought they would be mysteriously lifted into the sky, to return when the whites were gone.

The Oglala Sioux at the Pine Ridge reservation in South Dakota first heard of Wovoka and the Ghost Dance in the fall of 1889 from neighboring tribes, the Shoshoni and the Arapaho. They became greatly excited about the thought that soon all the whites would disappear, and that they would get their lands back. The Sioux also had an inordinate desire to see their dead, not only parents and other relatives, but warriors who died in battle, and the children who had succumbed to disease and malnutrition. A delegation headed by Good Thunder started out west, but apparently got no further than Fort Washakie in Wyoming, in the center of several reservations. But everywhere the Sioux heard the wonderful news of the Messiah and saw his dance being performed. Good Thunder's report when he returned home aroused a fervor of joyful excitement, and a second delegation, including Short Bull, Good Thunder, Yellow Knife, and Kicking Bear set off to meet the Messiah on the new railroad, which ran across Nevada and between the two great Indian reservations of Pyramid Lake and Walker Lake.

The delegates arrived at the reservation in April 1890, and began talking about the Messiah and the new dance which would end white domination and bring a return of the dead. Wovoka kept the various delegates with him for four or five days. They danced the new dance and heard him speak again and again of the coming millennium. He gave sacred red paint to the Indians. It was a deeply moving experience for the men who journeyed so far to hear him.

Dancing was taken up throughout the Sioux reservations. About half of the tribes' twenty-six thousand members—men, women, and children—joined in the movement. The local Indian agent, in a moment of fear and panic, arrested Good Thunder and two others, but the dancing continued. What was striking, and a fact the white authorities did not realize, was that the dance was universal, and was not confined to the warriors. It was not a war dance—in the past a common reason for dancing—but a dance of peace, in which the children joined their parents, and the wives their husbands. It was an intensely sacred rite, and unlike the dances of the past, it opened up the experience of the vision to all, not to the warriors alone.

Though there were many individual variations of the dance among the Indian tribes and nations that practiced it, in general it lasted four to six days, beginning with a period of fasting, often as long as twenty-four hours. At sunrise the men entered the sweat house for purification and then decorated themselves with the sacred red paint. Most of the Plains Indians wore the "ghost shirt," made of white cloth (buckskin was in short supply because the herds had been devastated). This again was unusual, because previous dances were performed with the upper body bare. The Shoshoni were among the earliest practitioners of the Ghost Dance, and influenced the Cheyenne, and from them the

White muslin shirts decorated with war and hunting symbols were worn by the Sioux during the Ghost Dance. The Sioux thought—tragically—that the shirts would protect them against the bullets of the white soldiers who attacked them. Many Sioux, women and children as well as the warriors, were found dead in these shirts. PHOTOGRAPH COURTESY OF MUSEUM OF THE AMERICAN INDIAN, HEYE FOUNDATION ghost shirt passed on to the Sioux, who, as with other aspects of the movement, gave a special interpretation, believing that the shirt rendered the wearer, man or woman, invulnerable to bullets and other weapons. When the government troops attacked the Sioux, this faith was to have tragic consequences. The Sioux decorated their shirts with various symbols, including those seen in visions. Many of the dancers in the Sioux tribes shed all metal objects during the dance, as though they were removing from themselves the stains of white influence. A few men, however, kept their rifles. A sweet smelling vernal grass (*Hierochloe*) was often rubbed on the body, and was also burned as incense.

By noon everyone would be ready for the dance. The Sioux and some other tribes placed a small tree in the center of the dance ground; other tribes used a pole, and others nothing. But noticeably absent was the fire around which dances had been performed in the past. The Sioux decorated the tree with feathers, stuffed animals, and stripes of cloth, and sometimes an American flag. The dance began with a short address by the leader, who told the participants about the chant and the movements. Sometimes as many as three hundred to four hundred persons would join the dance, each putting his or her hands on the shoulders of the person in front, and chanting, "Father, I come," while walking in a circle. A white woman, Mrs. Z. A. Parker, a teacher at the Pine Ridge reservation, saw the dance, and said at this point the dancers . . .

. . . stopped marching, but remained in the circle, and set up the most fearful, heart-piercing wails I ever heard—crying, moaning, groaning, and shrieking out their grief and naming over their departed friends and relatives, at the same time taking up handfuls of dust at their feet, washing their hands in it, and throwing it over their heads. Finally, they raised their eyes to heaven, their hands clasped high above their heads, and stood straight and perfectly still, invoking the power of the Great Spirit to allow them to see and talk with their people who had died.

After this, the dancers took each other's hands, fingers interlocked, and the great circle began to move as fast as possible around the

center in a great ring, bodies swaying, the Indians calling out in a
monotonous voice—

Father, I come;
Mother, I come;
Brother, I come;
Father, give us back our arrows.

This would be repeated endlessly until one after another would
break from the ring and fall down in a trance. Fully a quarter of
the dancers would soon be lying unconscious. Then the dancers
would stop and seat themselves in a circle on the ground, awaiting
the return of the others to consciousness. Then those who had entered trances would tell of their experiences. However, remarked
Mrs. Parker of the dancers she witnessed, "Not one in ten claimed
that he saw anything." But other reports differed, and there were
many accounts of Indians, not only Sioux, but members of many
other tribes, who "died" and went to heaven and saw their dead
friends and even brought back messages. Mooney was of the opinion that hypnosis had a large part in inducing trances.

The songs of the various tribes summarized with economy
of language and image the hopes and expectations of the Ghost
Dance. When Porcupine returned from Nevada he sang:

Our father has come,
Our father has come,
The earth has come,
The earth has come,
It is rising—Eyéyé!
It is rising—Eyéyé!
It is humming—Ahe'e'ye'!
It is humming—Ahe'e'ye'!

The song clearly referred to the Messiah and the new earth which
was approaching, making a humming or rolling sound (as of a
tidal wave?) as it came. An Arapaho song told about the misery of
the Indians:

Father, have pity on me;
Father, have pity on me;
I am crying for thirst;
I am crying for thirst;
All is gone—I have nothing to eat;
All is gone—I have nothing to eat.

A third song told of the rejection of the white man:

He'yoho'ho'! He'yoho'ho'!
The yellow hide, the white skin,
I have now put him aside—
I have now put him aside—I have no more sympathy with him,
I have no more sympathy with him.
He'yoho'ho'! He'yoho'ho'!

A Sioux song summarized the whole hope of the Dance—the return of the buffalo as promised by the father, Wovoka. The Eagle and the Crow were sacred birds.

The whole world is coming,
A nation is coming, a nation is coming.
The Eagle has brought the message to the tribe.
The father says so, the father says so.
Over the whole earth they are coming.
The buffalo are coming, the buffalo are coming.
The Crow has brought the message to the tribe,
The father says so, the father says so.

Each tribe had dozens if not hundreds of songs, and many referred to the visions seen by the Dancers. One Arapaho song began with the line, "With the bä'qati wheel I am gambling." The singer had visited the spirit world and found his old friends playing the game, which was done on a wheel. The game had become obsolete, but so many of the Plains tribes saw it in visions, that bä'qati was revived.

By August of 1890, there was dancing all over the Sioux

reservations, every few days. This month saw the movement at its peak, for almost the entire Sioux nation was seized with a desire to welcome the Messiah the moment He set foot on earth. The outburst alarmed the government agent at Pine Ridge, H. G. Galagher. He set out to find one of the dance leaders, a chief named White Bird, in order to learn what was happening. Galagher had fourteen Indian police with him, but before the party could reach White Bird's encampment, a group of twenty Sioux warriors, armed with Winchesters, sprang out of the bush and turned the government party back. News of the encounter and the unopposed Indian victory spread rapidly among Indians and whites. The excitement touched both races, but for different reasons. The Indians, who now danced regularly and everywhere, hoped to throw off the yoke of white oppression; the scattered settlers became fearful that their homes, their families, and their lives would be lost in an Indian uprising.

Troops were sent into the area. Galagher, who was a political appointee, with no knowledge of how to deal with the Indians under his supervision, was afraid to assert authority to stop the dancing—which of course he had no right to do anyway, as the Sioux were engaged in religious rites. He was soon replaced with another agent, D. R. Royer, also a political appointee and equally inexperienced. In the face of government vacillation, many Sioux began to look forward to the collapse of white interference, believing that the millennium promised by Wovoka was actually about to come. Besides the deep religious and mystical fervor which overwhelmed many people, a strong current of rebellion began to arise.

Press reports, from correspondents who knew nothing of the Ghost Dance and who had not visited the reservations, were published in the nation's newspapers, and alarmed the white populace and brought on government action. With whites' fears increasing daily as settlers exaggerated the originally peaceful Ghost Dance, with the Indians now dancing as much as possible in the expectation of the millennium, President Benjamin Harrison ordered the War Department to prepare for action. More troops were sent to the Sioux reservations in South Dakota under Major John R. Brooks. A considerable force was now garrisoned throughout Indian territory.

Wovoka attracted Indians from all over the continent with his message of the Ghost Dance. "All Indians must dance, everywhere," he said. "Keep on dancing. Pretty soon, next spring, Great Spirit come." And then the world would be fruitful for the Indians. COURTESY, SMITHSONIAN INSTITUTION

One of the leading Ghost Dancers among the Sioux, Red Cloud, said later:

The white men were frightened and called for soldiers. We had begged for life [from God], and the white men thought we wanted theirs. We heard that soldiers were coming. We did not fear. We hoped that we could tell them our troubles and get help. A white man said the soldiers meant to kill us. We did not believe it, but some were frightened and ran away to the Badlands.

In December, an Indian scout in the employ of the government, a half-breed named Louis Shangreaux (his first name is sometimes given as John in certain accounts), led a group of Sioux known as "friendlies" to visit some of the Dancers. The first settlement of Dancers—"hostiles" in the government terminology—agreed to stop dancing, then refused. The presence of the government-backed Indians brought the hostiles to hold a council, during which it was decided that a formal Ghost Dance would be held immediately.

The Indians formed a circle about the sacred tree and began their chant.

Of all the wild dancing I saw on Wounded Knee [said Shangreaux] this beat the record. People went into trances by the dozen, and the priests were kept busy relating the experiences of the fainters. Several remained in trances as long as twelve hours, and gave evidence of utter exhaustion when the leaders aroused them.

Short Bull said: "I see the Messiah coming from the West. He is riding in a plain-wagon drawn by two mules and looks very much like a black man. If he is our Messiah we are greatly fooled. Now I see him again, and he is an Indian. Ah, wait! I see him the third time and he is a white man. He tells me to send my children to school, to make large farms, and not to fight any more. Do not fight, my children, unless the soldiers first fire upon you."

People were so excited [continued Shangreaux] they trembled all over, their eyes rolled, and the muscles of their faces twitched. They were the most crazy Indians I ever saw.

The dance continued for thirty hours, with interruptions during which the friendlies and the hostiles talked. Shangreaux and the government Indians tried to persuade the Dancers to surrender. But Short Bull reiterated what the Indians had been saying for years: that the government always lied to them, had broken the treaties, had never given the rations that had been promised to replace the herds the whites had killed, that the Indians' guns and horses would be taken away, and that some of the Dancers would be put in prison.

One of the friendlies, No Neck, replied, "Think, my people, how foolish is this action! Do come in, and all will be well; remain out here and you will be killed." Short Bull replied that it was better to die as brave men, in obedience to the commands of the Good Spirit, than to live like cowards on the reservation.

No, we will not return. If we dance, our Good Spirit will protect us, and if all the dancers are sincere, the bullets of the soldiers will fall harmlessly to the ground without power to hurt. There is no army so powerful that it can contend with God. Therefore we are not afraid to remain here.

The dancing continued for two days. Then on the last, a Saturday, a general council was held, and one of the leaders, Two Strike, announced that he would surrender to the government along with 145 lodges or families. A riot almost broke out between the new friendlies and the Dancers, and Shangreaux thought he would be killed. But at last all the friendlies were able to start out for the reservation headquarters at White Clay, leaving behind 117 lodges of Dancers. After they had gone about two miles they looked back and saw Short Bull and the other Dancers following; they had also decided to surrender. But Short Bull soon became afraid of what would happen if he went to White Clay, and he and his people returned to their encampment, leaving the others to go to the reservations.

Now the first of a series of avoidable tragedies took place. The government forces, under a Major J. McLaughlin, decided that Sitting Bull, who was by now the most prominent Ghost Dance leader, must be arrested. A detachment of "loyal" Indian police, led by a Lieutenant Short Bull, with thirty-eight Sioux (four of them Sitting Bull's relatives) were sent after him. They found Sitting Bull in his lodge on the banks of the Grand River, and without difficultly, shortly before sunrise, arrested him. Sitting Bull dressed himself in his best robes, had his wives bring him his best horse, and was about to ride off with the police when a group of young men, all Ghost Dancers, crowded around him and began to taunt him for surrendering. Sitting Bull's son Crow Foot was particularly angry. Sitting Bull, seeing the seething crowd of his own people, called out to attack the police, and they fired. Almost at the same moment Lieutenant Bull Head fired at Sitting Bull, hitting him in the body, but was himself instantly shot. A second policeman also shot Sitting Bull in the head, and both the medicine man and the army officer fell to the ground, each mortally wounded. In the battle that followed, five other Indian police were killed, and eight Ghost Dancers, including Crow Foot, died. The police were able to withdraw with their dead.

Sitting Bull's death caused great excitement among the Sioux. Many uncommitted Indians joined the Ghost Dancers, convinced that no matter what they did, all would be killed. Scattered violence between Indians and whites continued through Christmas Day, with the whites gunning down stray Indians and their families like rabbits.

On December 28, a major cavalry force under Major Samuel Whiteside, of the Seventh Cavalry, went out to round up the remaining Ghost Dancers, who were led by Big Foot. But Big Foot, upon hearing of the death of Sitting Bull, had decided to come into the agency to surrender. Big Foot had 120 warriors and 230 women and children with him. En route Big Foot fell ill of pneumonia, began to hemorrhage, and was placed in a wagon. The Seventh Cavalry came across the Indians. Whiteside, through Louis Shangreaux, told Big Foot that they had to go to the army post at Wounded Knee Creek. Big Foot replied that he was on his way to Pine Ridge, where he thought his people would be safe. Whiteside replied that his orders were to bring them to Wounded Knee, and he told Shangreaux to disarm the Indians.

"Look here, Major," Shangreaux is said to have replied, "if

you try that, there is liable to be a fight, and if there is, you will kill the women and children and the men will get away." The Indians were not disarmed, but they agreed to go to the army encampment at Wounded Knee. They arrived there as the light was failing. It was bitterly cold, the creek was frozen, and there were snow and ice everywhere. During the night more cavalry came, under Colonel James W. Forsyth, who had orders to put the Indians on the Union Pacific train for shipment to the military prison in Omaha. The troops, who now numbered 430 men, set up four Hotchkiss machine guns pointed at the encamped Sioux, and they began to drink in celebration of their capture of Big Foot.

In the morning, breakfast rations were issued to the Indians, and then they were ordered to surrender their weapons. The guns were stacked in the center of the encampment. But Forsyth was not satisfied that he had all the weapons. The tents were searched, and axes, knives, and even tent stakes were piled by the guns. Then the Indians themselves were searched. Two more guns were found, one belonging to a young warrior named Black Coyote. Black Coyote, who was deaf and "a crazy man of very bad influence and in fact a nobody," according to Turning Hawk, a survivor of the massacre, protested that it was a new gun. The soldiers began to push him around. "If they had left him alone he was going to put his gun down where he should," said another Indian years later.

Nobody knew what happened at that point. A shot was heard, either from Black Coyote's gun, or from a soldier's gun. Immediately the soldiers opened fire on the Sioux, firing their carbines and the machine guns. Some of the warriors reached for their guns, others began to run, as did the women and children. Mooney said that the guns poured in two-pound explosives at the rate of fifty per minute, mowing down everything alive. In a few minutes 200 Indian men, women, and children were lying dead or wounded on the ground. The troops were said to have cried "Remember Custer" as they pursued those who fled, mainly the women and the children. Some of their bodies were found as far as two miles from the encampment. The cavalry lost 25 dead and 39 wounded, mainly from their own crossfire.

The young ethnologist James Mooney was present in South Dakota during the height of the Ghost dancing among the Sioux and recorded the ceremonies. These faded photographs are among his work. COURTESY, SMITHSONIAN INSTITUTION

The wounded Indians were later loaded into wagons and brought to the agency at Pine Ridge; the dead were left behind for the night. Quarters were scarce for the wounded survivors, four men and forty-seven women and children. A blizzard came, and they were left on the frozen ground for hours, until someone moved them into the Episcopal mission church. The benches were removed, hay was scattered on the floor, and the wounded could enjoy the Christmas greenery and the message of "Peace on Earth, Good Will to Men" hanging from the pulpit.

That was the end of the Ghost Dance among the Sioux. The ghost shirts had not protected them. The Ghost Dance survived a few years among other tribes, among them the Arapaho, Cheyenne, Caddo, Wichita, Pawnee, and Oto, but the expectations of an immediate millennium faded away, leaving as the main doctrine the hope of a sometime reunion with the departed in a better world. Wovoka went on exhibition as an attraction at the Midwinter Fair in San Francisco for a while, then retired to Walker Lake, where he died in 1932.

THE NATIVE AMERICAN CHURCH

The Ghost Dance was as dead as Sitting Bull, the one hundred and twenty braves, and the two hundred women and children who had perished at Wounded Knee. But the spirit that enlivened it and gave it hope was to continue among Indians in a different and more powerful form. This was the peyote movement, based upon a small cactus obtained in Mexico and the American Southwest. The cult, when fully matured, became the Native American Church, or one of its many variations of similar names. The key figure in the transformation of peyote from a healing practice into a viable religious movement was a mixed-blood Indian, John Wilson, of Delaware, Caddo, and French ancestry, born at Anardarko, a town on one of the Oklahoma reservations. Like many of the Indians of the late nineteenth century, John Wilson wandered about the Plains, from tribe to tribe, rootless and lost. It was a world in which traditional Indian values were seriously weakened if not destroyed, and white ways were encroaching on Indian culture and life. Wilson, then a Ghost Dance leader among the Caddo, was known to have attended a pantribal dance, one of the biggest on record, at Darlington, Oklahoma, in the fall of 1890, when the movement was at the height of its fervor. The dance was held under the leadership of a Comanche named Sitting Bull (not to be confused with the Sioux of the same name), and the Cheyennes also played an important part. Some of the Comanches were using peyote, and Wilson became interested (other accounts say he may have come across peyote on an earlier trip to Mexico). Wilson gathered a quantity of peyote buttons and with his wife he went off into the woods, camping by a creek.

Wilson spent six weeks in the wilderness, taking peyote and experiencing visions which turned him completely about and gave him the revelations which he was to pass on to others. He was then in his late forties, and up to that point had led a very dissolute life, drinking and gambling. With the discovery of peyote, all that changed. He took as many as fifteen buttons a day, studying the effects and experiencing visions.

The cactus, a small, low-growing, carrotlike plant, is botanically known as *Lophophora williamsii*. It has narcotic and hallucinogenic properties. It is not a pleasant drug to take, which may explain why in most cases it has been confined to ritual use. Its common physical effects are nausea and sometimes vomiting; the Indians take it under controlled conditions and primarily for religious purposes.

Because it seemed to possess divine qualities, it became a kind of deity in the minds of those who used it—thus as a deity it is "Peyote" (capitalized) but as the plant it is "peyote." Wilson, in his intense investigation, saw the button as both plant and deity.

"Peyote took pity on him," explained his nephew, George Anderson. During his period of seclusion and isolation, Wilson was transported in spirit by Peyote to the sky realm. There he saw the different figures in the sky and the celestial landmarks which represented the events in the life of Christ. He also saw the Spiritual Forces, the Moon, the Sun, and fire. He saw the grave of Christ, empty, "where Christ had rolled away the rocks at the door of the grave and risen to the sky."

Peyote showed him the "Road" which led from Christ's grave to the Moon in the Sky, the Road which Jesus had taken in His ascent. Peyote instructed him to walk on that Road for the rest of his life, advancing step by step as his knowledge increased through the use of peyote, remaining faithful to its teachings. Peyote gave him detailed instructions about the rites and rituals that were to be used in the observance of Peyote.

The visions continued in intensity. Wilson came to demand that Indians free themselves of the influence of western Christianity. His message reached out to other Indians, and he began to attract followers. He had been brought up as a Roman Catholic, and certain Catholic influences were apparent in his teachings. He rejected the Bible as a means of reaching God, a possible reflection of a Catholic attitude about the sacred book, for Catholics at that time had a hands-off attitude toward it. He may also have been rejecting a fundamentalist emphasis on the Bible. The Bible, said Wilson, had been given to the white man because he was guilty of slaying Jesus. It was the white man, not the Indian, who bore the burden of the Crucifixion. Thus the Bible was not meant for the Indian. Whites needed God's word through the Bible in order to gain the truth, but the Indians experienced truth through peyote. The Peyote Spirit he saw as an expression of Jesus.

Wilson composed songs, healed the sick, and was generally accepted as a prophet. Some Indians believe that Wilson will return to earth again, but Anderson denied that his uncle ever made such a claim. Still, some of the faithful pray directly to and through Wilson, and in some peyote lodges his portrait is placed near the peyote button and the Crucifix. Anderson was most specific about his uncle's not being divine. Wilson, he stressed, was not sent as Jesus was to fulfill a mission. Instead he was to show how to conduct worship so that diseases might be cured and injuries healed, and the body purged of the effects of sin. He was to lead Indians to the regions "above" where they could see both Peyote and the Creator.

Besides the visions in which he received the divine messages, Wilson communicated with God in other ways, notably, he told his followers, through an amulet of a bull's horn and red feathers which he wore about his neck. The Moon was central to his vision, and Wilson changed his name to Big Moon, or Moon Head—Nishkuntu in the Indian form. Consequently his version of the peyote cult was known as the Big Moon. He had converts throughout much of Oklahoma, many Indians among the Shawnee, the Seneca, the Quapaw, the Osage, and others. His death came about in a most unfortunate manner in 1891. He was on his way home from a mission to the Quapaw when his carriage was hit by a railroad train. But by that time peyote was firmly established among the Indians, and spreading steadily.

Upon Wilson's death his adopted son Lone Wolf took over, along with a Quapaw prophet, Victor Griffin. Other prophets arose and the Big Moon soon split into a number of sects, differing in rites and interpretations. Some shed all white and Christian influence, others saw themselves as a form of Christianity, if not *the true* Christianity as Jesus meant it to be. Among the sects were the Little Moon, the Western Moon, and the Road of the Sioux, none of which has survived.

The peyote movement, following diverse paths according to tribe and prophet, was joined by two men who were to have profound effects upon peyotism. One, a Winnebago, John Rave, had been converted to peyotism sometime around 1893–94, after many years of wandering about the Plains, visiting one tribe after another. As an adolescent he had failed the initiatory rites meant to induce the first visions in young men. He did not follow the ritual properly while he passed a night in isolation in the customary prayer and fasting. He had been noted as a restless and undisciplined youth. Now, barred from membership in the tribe's warrior caste, he set out to try to find communion with God in some other manner and in some other place. But he had no success. He joined a circus going abroad but became seasick and returned home where, ill and depressed, he became an alcoholic. He was also a heavy gambler and, as he later confessed, a selfish and dissolute man. "Before I ate peyote," Rave told the anthropologist Paul Radin, who recorded his odyssey, "my heart was filled with murderous thoughts. I wanted to kill my brother and sister." His drinking and wanton life brought him almost to the point of insanity, and when he came across a peyote community in Oklahoma he joined the ceremony.

In the middle of the night we were to eat peyote. We ate it and I also did. It was the middle of the night when I became frightened, for a live thing seemed to have entered me. "Why did I do it?" I thought to myself. "I should not have done it, for right at the beginning I have harmed myself. Indeed I should not have done it. I am sure it will injure me. The best thing will be for me to vomit it up."

He thought he was going to die. He saw a big snake crawling toward him. But he took peyote again a second night, with almost equally bad visions. A hideous creature with legs and arms and a tail pointed like a spear tried to kill him. But the third night was different for Rave.

I saw God. To God living up above, our Father, I prayed. Have mercy upon me! Give me knowledge that I may not say and do evil things! To you, O God, I am trying to pray. Do Thou, O Son of God help me too. This religion let me know. Help me, O Medicine! Grandfather, help me! Let me know thy religion!

A fourth vision seemed to sum up his revelation. In this he found the true source of knowledge.

I seemed to see everything clearly. O Medicine, grandfather, most assuredly you are holy. Through all the years that I have lived on earth, I now realize that I had never known anything so holy. Now, for the first time, I knew it.

Rave told Radin:

Now I know that I had taken the wrong road [before his conversion] and I shall never take it again. I was like blind and deaf . . . the Peyote is life, the only life, and only by eating peyote will you learn what is truly holy.

Rave soon had followers. He believed peyote had enormous curative powers—it not only cured alcoholism but tuberculosis, wounds, and other ailments. He introduced some Christian elements into his ceremony, notably public confession in the new faith and public confession of sins. Sixteen years after his conversion Rave came across another Winnebago who was especially sensitive to peyote. This was Albert Hensley, a tribal prophet. Hensley had been partaking of peyote for a number of years, and had worked out an amalgam of traditional tribal and Christian beliefs, with a heavy emphasis on the Bible. Many of the peyote users in Oklahoma already had used the Bible in their rituals, but more as a superstition than for its contents. Hensley translated parts of the Bible into Winnebago, using the texts alternately with peyote songs. Also, he placed the peyote button atop the Bible in token of the intimate relationship of the two, for he believed that Christianity had accepted and continued rites of Indian origin, which he proved by his choice of biblical passages—he could, for example, equate Christ's anguished prayer at night in the Garden of Gethsemane with the nighttime peyote rites.

Hensley was convinced that peyote was the great unifying force for the Indians and for a pan-Indian movement. "You Indians are fighting each other," he would warn the various tribes he met, "and it is in order to stop this that you must now shake hands and partake of food together." Moreover, he developed a ritual which could be followed by all, of whatever tribe, and he urged his hearers to go forth and preach to all the Indian nations.

Dozens of other prophets arose to spread the word of peyote, some part of the mainstream, others isolated in distant areas or on reservations which had little contact with other Indians. Ben Lancaster (also called Chief Gray Horse), Leo Okio, Raymond Lone Bear, Johnny Wright, and Elk Hair are some of the more famous leaders. Elk Hair was the prophet of the Little Moon sect; he stressed the healing aspects of peyote.

The peyote movement took on a more orthodox form in

the hands of Jonathan Koshiway. He was enrolled in the Oto tribe, his mother's, but also had Sauk and Fox in his immediate ancestry. He had been an Indian evangelist for the Mormons in northeast Kansas, but he was also influenced by the Jehovah's Witnesses, then known as the Russellites. Koshiway picked up some of the Witnesses' millennial doctrines, along with their hostility to formal government. At the same time he borrowed whatever seemed applicable from the more orthodox forms of Christianity. He equated the bread and wine of the Eucharistic sacrifice with peyote, and found the traditional canonical virtues of Christianity—love, honor, and so on—to be the same as those followed by Indians. In 1914, in Red Rock, Oklahoma, his movement was formally incorporated as the First-born Church of Christ. Koshiway and 410 other Indians signed the papers. Meanwhile there had been other attempts at uniting the peyotists into a national unit. A few years earlier the Omaha had founded the American Indian Church Brother Association, and there was the Kiowa United American Church. A group of mescal eaters at Winnebago, Nebraska, had formed the Union Church.

Eventually members of the various organizations met to pull the scattered groups together, as well as to fight attempts by federal and state agencies to put down peyotism among Indians as a dangerous custom. At Cheyenne, Oklahoma, a group of Oto, Kiowa, and Arapaho met, along with the anthropologist James Mooney, to discuss the ever-increasing danger that peyote would be legislated out of existence. The conference was attended by Koshiway, who tried to persuade the delegates to come into the First-born Church of Christ. There was much objection to the "white-sounding" name of the organization, and the result was the forming of the Native American Church. Koshiway left his own organization and became a leading member of the new movement, though he had to play a lesser role than in his original church.

The Native American Church was formally organized in 1918 in Oklahoma City, and a broad spectrum of tribes joined in signing the papers. Since then, it has continued to grow and flourish, though there are branches and minor schisms and recently founded rivals. But today peyotism is perhaps the most firmly established and widespread form of religion among the American Indian. Peyotism even inspired a black peyote church, the Negro Church of the First-born, founded by a man named John Jamison, who had grown up among Indians in Oklahoma and spoke several Indian languages. Jamison closely followed the Indian rites, but many of the younger Indians resented blacks taking up the "old Indian religion," and the church did not survive his death in 1926.

Though peyotism is first and foremost an Indian cult, it is also in part "Christian." Among the Mexican tribes, who of course were the first to use it, there are only superficial signs of Christian influence. The Mexican Indians use peyote—so it is assumed by anthropologists—much as they have for hundreds if not thousands of years. But as peyote passed northward up to the Apache and then to the Plains tribes and beyond, it became entwined with Christian elements. The rites themselves ebbed and flowed as various prophets arose, either to blend with the Christianity of their childhood mission education, or to deny them and try to return to what they considered the original Indian ways. But generally Christianity played a part in some form or other, though in ways that made the orthodox uneasy.

Among the Arapaho and Winnebago, the peyote leader represents Adam, and a woman dressed in finery is the New Jerusalem—the heavenly bride waiting for the bridegroom. A cup of water shared by both symbolizes the fact that they are about to become One; the water represents God's gift of His holiness. At the rites, corn represents the feast on the day of Judgment, fruit is the fruit of the Tree of Life, and meat is the message of Jesus. Those who accept the fruit are the saved. Among the Winnebago, Quapaw, and Osage, the peyote leader represents the Father, the drummer is the Son, and the cedar-man is the Holy Ghost. The Oto shapes the ashes of the ritual fire into a bird form, to represent the Holy Spirit descending when Jesus was baptized ("the Holy Spirit, like an eagle with good eyes, you can't fool it"). The fire in the tepee is like the fire through which God spoke to Moses. And peyote is like a "telescope" through which you can see God. The Delaware see the twin piles of ashes as Christ's lungs, while among the Osage one pile is Christ's grave, the other John Wilson's. And so on. The imagery is unbounded and poetic and pertinent to the message that peyote saves, that peyotism is the original religion, bestowed by God upon His Chosen People, the Indians, preservers of the sacred Truth which the whites desecrated and abandoned.

One of the great peyote leaders, the Comanche chief Quanah Parker, said:

The white man goes to his church house and talks about Jesus, but the Indian goes into his tipi and talks to Jesus.

The Indian knows that peyote is the original religion. "Christ was born only several hundred years ago, not when the world was created, like peyote," says a Shawnee. A Kickapoo comments: "We had medicine bags before Jesus was born over in Bethlehem, in the old country."

8

THE MUSLIMS

A "MESSENGER" APPEARED IN THE POVERTY-STRICKEN black ghetto of Detroit, a seller of silks and other goods. The year was 1930, and the Depression, which had shattered America's economy, had hit blacks harder than others. The silk seller identified himself as a "brother from the East." He called himself Wallace D. Fard, but he also had a variety of other names: W. D. Fard, Wali Farrad, Farrad Muhammad, F. Muhammad Ali, and also Professor Ford. People who remember him today describe him as "a small, light, brown-skinned man." His origins were a mystery, and may never be known. He told people, "I come from the Holy City of Mecca. More about myself I will not tell you yet, for the time has not yet come. I am your brother. You have not seen me in the royal robes." Such statements echoed some of the words of Jesus. Some people believed that Fard was the son of wealthy parents of the Prophet Muhammad's own clan, the Koreish (or Quraish); however, others said he was a Jamaican negro whose father was a Muslim from Syria. Others claimed that he was a Palestinian who had been involved in racial movements in India, South Africa, and England. When the Detroit police picked him up for questioning, Fard informed them that he was "the Supreme Ruler of the Universe."

That Fard had some special sense of his mission is seen in the names he used. In Arabic, "Walī" means "the Saint," "the Man of God," while "Wālī" is "the Victorious." "Fard" is "the Singular," "the Unusual." Both terms are used mystically, especially by the Sufis, who follow an inner teaching of Islamic esotericism. Thus "Wali Fard" means "the Sainted Chosen One." Strangely enough, the significance of Fard's name is overlooked in American black Muslim literature and teachings.

Fard warned negroes (as blacks were then called) against eating "filthy pig" and other "wrong foods" that blacks often ate, for either they were transgressing the law of Allah or were eating the foods of the whites who enslaved them. He held meetings in their poor homes, preaching a message of salvation taken from both the Quran and the Bible, and told his listeners, all blacks, that the Christian name "God" was wrong, that "Allah" was proper, and that negroes in America were the Lost Sheep, direct descendants of the Muslims, separated for four hundred years from the nation of Islam, to which all negroes belong by birth. Fard said that it was his role to come to redeem the negro and return him to his true religion.

He was a man of mystery, but his message went right to the hearts of his listeners, blacks who were not only suffering the worst of the Depression but who had had a long history of oppression behind them. Even in the decade or so before Fard's appearance, tremendous atrocities against blacks had been the ordinary course of events. In 1919, the year after World War I had ended—

a "war to save democracy"—seventy blacks had been lynched, some still in the uniforms they had worn as soldiers in the American army. Eleven blacks had been burned alive that year. During the summer of 1919, twenty-five race riots had erupted in America. In one, in Chicago, 38 people were killed and 537 injured in thirteen days during which whites rampaged through black areas. Succeeding years were no better.

Fard's teachings were an awakening to many of Detroit's poverty-stricken blacks. They were told that the black people, the children of Allah, God, were "Gods themselves." There was no heaven in the sky, no hell in the ground as the Bible said. But Fard explained that both heaven and hell were conditions on earth, and that blacks had lived for four hundred years in hell on earth. The devil himself lived on earth—the white race was the blue-eyed devil. Fard's mission was to lead the blacks back to heaven, among their own kind, the Muslims.

This was to take place according to tenets held by virtually all religions. At the Last Day, or the End of Time, Allah would come to resurrect the Lost Sheep to separate them from their enemies and restore them to their own people. Prophecy, stated Fard, referred to the Finder and Savior of the Lost Sheep as the Son of Man, or God in Person, or the Lifegiver, the Redeemer, the Messiah. By whatever name, He will come as lightning from the east and appear in the west. The great faiths—Judaism, Christianity, and Islam—have different names for this savior—the Messiah, the Christ, the Mahdi.

One of Fard's most receptive disciples was a man in his early forties named Elijah Poole. Poole was born of a poor family in rural Georgia. His father was a Baptist preacher who worked as a farm hand. Poole came to Detroit in 1923 after a run-in with a white farmer made him realize that he could no longer live in the South. He joined Fard's movement in 1931, and quickly rose to a major position in the tiny movement. He was elected Supreme Minister over the other Muslim ministers, and his importance resulted in much resentment from men Poole called "hypocrites." Poole had been renamed Elijah Muhammad, because Fard was replacing blacks' "white" names with Muslim names. Many people—such as the famous convert Malcolm Little—received an X as their last name. The X symbolized the unknown African name that had been replaced by the name some blue-eyed white devil had imposed on his black slaves.

To Elijah Muhammad, as to others who joined the Muslim movement, Fard was the Savior. Malcolm X, in his autobiography, reports a conversation with Muhammad about Fard.

Mr. Muhammad told me that one evening he had a revelation that Master W. D. Fard represented the fulfillment of the prophecy [concerning the savior of mankind].

"I asked Him," said Mr. Muhammad, "who are you, and what is your real name? And He said, 'I am The One the world has been looking for to come for the past two thousand years.'

"I said to Him again," said Mr. Muhammad, "what is your true name? And then He said, 'My name is Mahdi. I came to guide you into the right path.' "

Fard was not the only messiah to appear before blacks to offer an alternative to Christianity. Others in the black communities of the big cities had turned away from what they called the religion of the slaveholders, believing that Christianity did not offer an authentic Way for blacks. There was, for example, a group called the Commandment Keepers, a black Jewish sect which stated that all so-called negroes were of Hebrew stock and could trace their ancestry back to King Menelik I of Ethiopia who, they believed, was the son of King Solomon and the Queen of Sheba. The Commandment Keepers had been founded in Harlem in 1919 by a man named Wentworth David Matthew, a native of Nigeria, who said he was a Fallah or Ethiopian Jew and had received his rabbinical certificate in Cincinnati and Berlin. (In 1927, the Commandment Keepers absorbed a smaller group of black Jews with similar tenets founded by a West Indian black, Rabbi Joseph Ford, who went off to Ethiopia, never to return.) Rabbi Matthew claimed 3,300 followers in Harlem and an equal number in temples in major black areas as far west as Salt Lake City. At the height of their popularity, the Commandment Keepers had a home for the aged, operated several cigar and stationery stores and other small businesses, and were working on plans for an agricultural project on Long Island.

At least two black sects in Harlem claimed direct descent from Adam, who, they stated authoritatively, was a negro. They believed that the black race had once been supreme on earth. One sect was the House of Israel, a black Jewish movement, the other the Moorish Science Temple, which followed Islam. Both sects ran schools in which the Ethiopian language was taught, and they claimed that they were enslaved by the white race since their ancient tongue was not a subject in the public schools.

In 1934, Fard mysteriously disappeared. No trace of him was ever found, either by his followers or the police. It was as if he had ascended into the heavens. With the Prophet and "Savior" gone, Elijah Muhammad took over the Muslim movement. It grew steadily as he expounded the teachings he had received from Master Fard. Elijah Muhammad said he had been favored with private instructions from Fard and that he had "heard things never revealed to others." (It is now difficult to tell whether certain doctrines are Fard's, or Muhammad's.) One of the most important revelations to the Detroit Muslims is the account of how the white man came to the planet Earth. The Muslims called the story "Yacub's History."

According to the Detroit Muslims, the first humans were a black people, who founded the Holy City of Mecca. Among this black race were twenty-four wise scientists, one of whom developed feelings of resentment to the others. This man created the especially strong black tribe of Shabazz, from which the so-called American negroes, or blacks, descended. Some 6,600 years ago, in a polarization between those who were satisfied—some 70 percent—and the minority who were not, there was born a Mr. Yacub of the dissatisfied group. He was born to create trouble, to break the peace, and to murder. Because of the size of his skull, he was known as "the big-head scientist," and he was especially gifted in many fields, including genetics.

Mr. Yacub began preaching his message of dissatisfaction in the streets of Mecca, gaining so many converts that the authorities decided to exile Yacub and his followers. The scientist and 59,999 disciples were exiled to the island of Patmos, the island where John received the message contained in the Book of Revelation.

As revenge, Mr. Yacub decided to create a devil race upon the earth, a bleached-out white race of people. As a scientist, Yacub knew that black man—the only kind of man on earth—contained two genes, black and brown. The brown gene was dormant, recessive, and weaker, being the lighter in color. By selective breeding, Yacub knew that he could produce successively lighter and lighter stages of man. The result would be people who, as they became lighter and weaker, were also more susceptible to wickedness and evil. The result would be the bleached-out white race of devils.

As children were born among the exiles in Patmos, Yacub had all the black children killed, keeping only the brown-skinned babies. As they grew up, only brown and brown were permitted to marry. Mr. Yacub died at the age of 152, leaving instructions for his assistants to follow. Two hundred years were needed to eliminate all the black people, leaving only browns. Another two hundred years were needed to produce a race of red-skins and breed out the browns. The reds were bred over the next two hundred years to produce yellow-skins. And two hundred years later the white race had been created. Thus on Patmos there were nothing but blond, pale-skinned, cold-blue-eyed devils—savages, nude and shameless; hairy, like animals, who walked on all fours and lived in trees.

Some six hundred years later, the whites were able to return to the mainland, and here through their wiles and their lies they set the black people to fighting among themselves, thus turning a peaceful heaven on earth into a hell torn by quarreling and fighting.

But the blacks soon realized what the whites were doing to them. Elijah Muhammad taught that the blacks rounded up the white devils and exiled them to the caves of Europe, where they spent two thousand years in savagery, fighting and living like animals. It was then that Allah raised up Moses to civilize them and bring them out of their caves. These first people were the biblical

Jews. The Books of Moses, a work known in the past and now missing, Muhammad said, taught that the devil white race would rule for six thousand years, until a Savior appeared, in the present age, born of the original black people of the ancient past, some of whom had been brought to North America as slaves where they could learn firsthand the nature of the white devil.

In Muhammad's cosmogony, "the greatest and mightiest God who appeared on earth was Master W. D. Fard." He came from east to west, to North America, when both history and prophecy were coming to fulfillment, as the nonwhite peoples of the world began to arise, and as the devil white civilization, the condemned of Allah, was destroying itself through its own devilish nature. Fard himself, half black, half white, could be accepted by blacks, yet move among whites undiscovered in order to understand and judge his people's enemies.

Elijah Muhammad's version of what Fard taught has been widely criticized by more traditional Muslims, especially those of Mecca. It has been considerably muted in recent years, especially after the death of the Supreme Minister in 1975. But in the early years of the Community it had an electrifying effect upon blacks who were exposed to it, and it helped put their years of oppression and misery into perspective.

The Community continued to grow through the 1930s under Muhammad's leadership. World War II broke out on December 7, 1941, and a few months later Elijah Muhammad was arrested on a charge of draft-dodging, though at forty-two he was a year over the age for military service. He was sentenced to prison for five years. Muslim critics state that he also counseled younger Muslims not to serve, which was a federal offense in itself. He was released from prison a year after the war ended, and he returned to the Community, the "Lost-Found Nation of Islam in North America."

MALCOLM X
Elijah Muhammad's group looked as if it would be but one of a large number of black religious movements in the United States,

surviving in a tenuous role in black society in which blacks were trying to come to grips with the often demeaning problem of existing in a world that really did not want them. Black Christian churches, trying to find a black way to God, proliferated, and still do, and Islam had been a possible solution for others than Elijah Muhammad. However, the conversion of a professional criminal, Malcolm Little, brought an unsuspected power and a true charisma to the Community.

Little was born in Omaha in 1935. His father was a Baptist minister who followed the teachings of Marcus Garvey's Universal Negro Improvement Association and was convinced that the black man would never be free in America and must return to his homeland, Africa. Three of the minister's brothers had been killed by whites, one in a lynching. Later the Reverend Little himself was killed by whites and another brother shot by northern police. While Malcolm's mother was carrying him, the Ku Klux Klan rode up to their house on horseback and warned her that her husband, who was then out of town, must leave Omaha. Little moved his family to Milwaukee and then to Lansing, Michigan. He continued to preach for Garvey, and was denounced by blacks as well as whites. In 1929, whites burned down his house. Finally the Littles moved to the countryside outside Lansing, to a house which the pastor had built himself.

Young Malcolm was confined to a house of detention for a schoolboy prank against a white teacher. When he was in the eighth grade he was transferred to Boston in the custody of a sister, and from there on he drifted into a life of crime, which he detailed in his moving and very dramatic autobiography. In New York's Harlem he was a pimp, a drug peddler, and a thief. He was finally arrested in Boston on a charge of burglary—he had headed a gang using white girls to case possible sites—and was convicted to ten years in prison, serving first in Charleston, and then in the more liberal Norfolk Prison Colony in Massachusetts. It was in Norfolk that he became a Muslim. His brothers and sisters in Detroit and Chicago had already been converted. At Norfolk, his brother Reginald told him about Allah during a visit, and that "the white man is the devil—without exception."

You don't even know who you are [said Reginald]. You don't even know, the white devil has hidden it from you, that you are of a race of people of ancient civilizations, and riches and gold and kings. You don't even know your true family name, you wouldn't recognize your true language if you heard it. You have been cut off by the devil white man from all true knowledge of your own kind. You have been a victim of the evil of the devil white man ever since he murdered and raped and stole you from your native land in the seeds of your forefathers. . . .

Reginald told Malcolm of the "Honorable Elijah Muhammad," a small gentle man whom they sometimes called the "Messenger of Allah," and "a black man like us." Reginald also told his brother of The Lost-Found Nation of Islam in the wilderness of North America, of the need to worship Allah, and to give up pork, narcotics, tobacco, and liquor. "The key to a Muslim," Malcolm heard over and over from his brothers and sisters, "is submission, the attunement of one toward Allah."

Malcolm Little daily wrote to Elijah Muhammad, sometimes twice a day, and began to study Islam and to read everything possible in the Norfolk prison library. He was undergoing an intense program of self-improvement. He took up debating and prayed daily to Allah. At this point Malcolm experienced what might be described as a vision. One night as he lay on his prison cot, he became aware of a man sitting in the chair beside him. The man was wearing a dark suit, he had skin of an intermediate tone, and oily black hair. Malcolm stared at him for a while, and then the figure was gone. Little learned later that his vision was of Master W. D. Fard, "the Messiah."

Little was transferred back to the Charleston prison, apparently for his Muslim activities, and was finally released in 1952. He went back to Detroit where he got a job in a furniture store managed by his brother Wilfrid. In his brother's home he learned the proper way to follow the Muslim ritual of prayer, said five times a day by the faithful, and joined the Detroit Temple Number One. He met Elijah Muhammad for the first time and became an active proselytizer. His name was changed from Malcolm Little to

Malcolm X, thus erasing the shame of bearing a former slave-holder's name. Malcolm X worked for a while in a factory, and then on an automobile assembly line. But soon he began to practice as a full-time Muslim minister, and shortly became famous as the best known of the members of the Nation of Islam in the West. Muslim preaching has stressed the plight of blacks rather than religious doctrine—in fact, the Oneness of Allah and devotion to Him as more traditional forms of Islam preaching did not occupy the minds and souls of Elijah Muhammad's followers to the extent that they do in more orthodox communities. However, Malcolm X's speeches went directly to the heart of black-white relationships.

I charge the white man with being the greatest liar on earth! I charge the white man with being the greatest drunkard on earth. . . . I charge the white man with being the greatest gambler on earth. I charge the white man . . . with being the greatest peace-breaker on earth. I charge the white man with being the greatest adulterer on earth. I charge the white man with being the greatest robber on earth. I charge the white man with being the greatest trouble-maker on earth.

These words were spoken before a black jury in a mock trial in Boston, and the verdict was guilty as charged.

The Muslim Community contains a great number of ex-prisoners, many of them converted during their terms. Unlike the white and Christian world, where ex-convicts are looked upon with a mixture of fear, suspicion, and contempt, the Community has welcomed even the most unregenerate and set about the work of rehabilitation. Malcolm said:

They say a man should never be condemned or tried twice for the same crime once he has paid the penalty. Yet when a man goes to prison and pays his debt to society, when he comes out he is still looked upon as a criminal. . . . Well, Mr. Muhammad has succeeded there where Western Christianity has failed. When a man becomes a Muslim, it doesn't make any difference what he was doing before as long as he has stopped doing this. He is looked upon with honor and respect and is not judged for what he was doing yesterday. And this, I think, explains why we have so many men who were in prison following Mr. Muhammad today.

Accepting Islam means a major change in an individual's life, whether for a person who has avoided trouble or for a former criminal. Again, Malcolm said:

It is a known fact, and sociologists agree, that when a man becomes a follower of Mr. Muhammad, no matter how bad his morals or habits were, he immediately takes upon himself a pronounced change which everyone admits. He [Mr. Muhammad] stops them from being dope addicts. He stops them from being alcoholics; alcohol is a curse on the so-called negroes. He has taken men who were thieves, who broke the law—men who were in prison—and reformed them so that no more do they stray, no more do they commit crimes against the government. I should like to think that this government would thank Mr. Muhammad for doing what it has failed to do toward rehabilitating men who have been classed as hardened criminals. . . . The psychologists and the penologists—all the sociologists—admit that crime is on the increase, in prison and out. Yet when the Black Man who is a hardened criminal hears the teachings of Mr. Muhammad, immediately he makes an about-face. Where the warden couldn't straighten him out through solitary confinement, as soon as he becomes a Muslim, he begins to become a model prisoner right in that institution, far more than whites or so-called negroes who confess Christianity.

By stressing political and economic problems, as well as the distinctness of color, Muhammad and Malcolm X made their version of Islam a radically different religion from what Muslims of the Arab countries had taken to be orthodox belief. Among the American Muslims there was then little of the emphasis on faith, prayer, Allah Himself, or the Islamic saints, messengers, and prophets that are so much a part of orthodox Islam. Though American Muslims in the black ghettos mentioned Allah, it was with the emphasis on His blackness rather than on His divine aspects. Yet the Community quietly observed Islamic rituals and codes so far as they knew about them and understood them. Members prayed five times a day, facing Mecca, after a ritual cleansing of their bodies. They gave the *zakat*, or tithe, to the best of their abilities. Members were exhorted to self-improvement, neatness, probity, and exemplary behavior in sexual matters. Certain foods were proscribed according to Muslim law.

The Muslims attained national prominence in 1959 through a series of unexpected events. One was a television program reported by Mike Wallace, with the aid of Louis Lomax, a black journalist. The program was entitled "The Hate that Hate Produced." Malcolm X charged that through selective editing, it showed what could be taken to be Muslim violence, unnecessary anger, and mistrust of whites. It was a distorted, and untrue version of what the black Islamic Community actually believed and practiced. Shortly after that a book by the black sociologist C. Eric Lincoln, *The Black Muslims in America*, added further to the negative image. Lincoln's work was a rather flat sociological tract, though it was marred by unprofessional value judgments ("racist sect," "militant," "sinister," "ominous" are but a few). It added to the general apprehension over a growing organization of blacks totally dedicated to what seemed to be an alien religion—Islam—and a belief that whites are not to be trusted and are in fact "blue-eyed devils." Lincoln's work gave the Community the label "Black Muslims," one which has stuck, though the members themselves reject it, insisting that all blacks are Muslim by origin.

The Muslims soon became popular subjects for magazine articles and newspaper features, which all too often stressed the scare features of the movement. Malcolm X gained widespread notoriety on television talk shows where, along with attempts to straighten the record for the audiences, he also contributed a great amount of material that served to frighten whites and many blacks about the true objectives of the Muslims. Later readings in a calmer atmosphere showed that his statements were not so controversial, and they made a great deal of sense under the circumstances. But among blacks, especially those at the bottom of the social scale, the Muslims continued to attract converts. By 1961, plans were announced for a twenty-million-dollar Islamic center to be built in Chicago. Various businesses established by Elijah Muhammad to help support the Muslim work grew in size.

Malcolm X appeared to be Muhammad's favorite disciple, and his possible successor. The Supreme Minister's health was bad, and he made a special point in emphasizing his faith in Malcolm. There was much intra-Community jealousy of Malcolm, to the point where he received veiled threats. Then a crisis arose between Malcolm and Muhammad. Malcolm's brother Reginald, who had converted him, had broken with the Muslims as the result of his earlier belief that Muhammad had been engaged in rather scandalous acts. Malcolm refused to listen to his brother. Muhammad excommunicated Reginald, and Malcolm told his own brother that he was no longer welcome among the Muslims. Yet rumors about Muhammad's involvement with certain women continued. Various members of the Community asked Malcolm to act. He spoke to several women said to be involved with the Supreme Leader, and they confirmed the reports.

Malcolm, who followed the utmost honesty in personal and public life since his conversion, asked Muhammad for a meeting. The confrontation took place in Phoenix, Arizona, in April 1963. Muhammad did not deny the rumors but told Malcolm he was merely fulfilling prophecy.

I'm David [said Muhammad]. When you read about how David took another man's wife, I'm that David. You read about Noah, who got drunk—that's me. You read about Lot, who went and laid up with his own daughters. I have to fulfill all of those things.

With the revelation of this "prophecy," Malcolm knew that the Muslims were in a precarious situation, and he decided that he must warn some of the other ministers. But the situation was suddenly taken out of his hands with his unfortunate, misunderstood remarks about the assassination of President John F. Kennedy in

Dallas in November the same year. He had been preaching a sermon called "God's Judgment of White America," about "how the hypocritical American white man was reaping what he had sowed." Reporters asked him about Kennedy's murder.

Without a second thought I said what I honestly felt—that it was, as I saw it, a case of "the chickens coming home to roost." I said that the hate in white men had not stopped with the killing of defenseless black people, but that hate, allowed to spread unchecked, finally had struck down this country's Chief of State. I said it was the same thing that happened to Medgar Evers, with Patrice Lumumba, with Madame Nhu's husband.

Newspaper headlines and radio and television broadcasts took the comments out of context, stressing that the "Black Muslims' Malcolm X had said, 'Chickens Come Home to Roost.' " It sounded as if Malcolm had condoned the murder of the president.

The country loved this man, Elijah Muhammad told Malcolm when they met the next day. A blunder like that could make it hard for Muslims. And he suspended Malcolm for ninety days. Malcolm accepted the censure but was shocked and hurt to know that Muhammad had also denounced him publicly.

A crisis then developed. Malcolm believed that a long-planned attempt to get rid of him because of his popularity was developing. He reported attempts on his life. The Muslims were split over the controversy, and Malcolm decided that rather than remain silent as a member of the Nation of Islam—an organization in which his life was clearly in danger—he would start afresh with another organization. He announced the formation of a new temple in New York, known as Muslim Mosque, Inc. Then, with the help of his sister Ella, he set off on the pilgrimage to Mecca, the *hajj* which is the duty of every able-bodied male Muslim to make at least once in a lifetime.

Malcolm X's pilgrimage to the holy city of all Islam is one of the most moving chapters in his autobiography. He was welcomed by Muslims of all types and races and colors, and for the first time he saw the brotherhood of Islam, joined not by race, for all the races of the world are encompassed by Islam, but by the unity of mankind in the Oneness of Allah. He began to appraise the "white man."

"White man," as commonly used, means complexion only. In America, "white man" meant specific attitudes and actions toward the black man and toward all other nonwhite men. But in the Muslim world, I had seen that men with white complexions were more genuinely brotherly than anyone else ever had been.

This insight was a radical alteration in his outlook about "whites."

He visited the sacred shrines, and then journeyed on to several African countries, where he was welcomed as a fellow Muslim and as a black working to help American blacks. Malcolm returned home with the message of the all-encompassing unity of Islam, the statement that whites as well as blacks could be equal members of the Muslim brotherhood. Constantly he heard of threats against his life, and on February 6, 1963, he broke his silence on criticisms of his former associates in the Muslims and charged that "my death has been ordered by higher-ups in the movement." He reported attempts on his life in Los Angeles, and again at his home in East Elmhurst, Long Island. On February 21, Malcolm, aged thirty-nine, was shot to death as he began a speech at a rally in Harlem at the Audobon Ballroom by a twenty-two-year-old black named Thomas Hagan. Police rescued the murderer from the crowd of followers, who would have beaten and kicked him to death.

Malcolm's death almost united the sundered Muslims. His own followers, including his blood brothers, who were Muslim ministers, pleaded for the unity of all at a great meeting attended by Muslims from both groups. But Elijah Muhammad said, "He was a star that went astray." He added, "We stand beside the grave of a hypocrite." Then: "Who was he leading? Who was he teaching? He has no truth! We didn't want to kill Malcolm! His foolish teaching brought him to his own end! I am not going to let the crackpots destroy the good things Allah sent to you and me!"

THE NEW MUSLIMS

In February 1975, Elijah Muhammad died. His place was taken by his sixth son, Wallace Deen Muhammad. The son had often been estranged from his father over policies and tactics, and for a while had supported Malcolm X in trying to get Elijah Muhammad to abandon his sexual affairs. In the days following the transition, the Community was in chaos as Wallace tried to reorganize. There is reported to have been looting and theft of Muslim properties by some of the members. But Wallace soon gained control. In a series of forceful moves, he changed the "Black Muslims" into a quite traditional, middle-of-the-road Islamic group, throwing out the strange and even rabid doctrines that Wallace Fard and Elijah Muhammad had taught in order to attract members.

In a most astounding move, Wallace Muhammad criticized the movement's founder. Though he could credit Fard with being "the cause for the existence of the World Community of al-Islam in the West," he also said that Fard used "tricks and strange mystical teaching to gather followers." Fard's doctrine of "Yacub's grafted devil, the skunk of the planet Earth" and the "Island of Patmos madness" . . . "really was a burden on all of us. I don't think any of us ever digested that to our satisfaction, because we couldn't understand how the colored man became the white man." However, Fard meant well in trying to reach the down-trodden in Detroit, the uneducated, and the unemployed. What Fard taught, says Wallace Muhammad today, was not true Islam. And: "I am a Muslim. I don't believe that God is going to reveal a new religion. I believe we have enough religion. We just need to understand the original religion."

Today the World Community of al-Islam in the West is a solidly based, widely respected branch of international Islam. Wallace Muhammad has sold off many of the far-flung businesses started by his father and established the Community on a sound financial base. Gone are the diatribes against the blue-eyed devil; in fact, whites—now called caucasians in an attempt to avoid racist labels (as blacks are now Bilalians, after the first black convert to Islam in the seventh century A.D.)—are encouraged to join, and there are a few of them among the Muslims. Nearly a quarter of a million American blacks, or Bilalians (for all blacks are considered Bilalians), can be comfortably counted among the members. The American Muslims are accepted as orthodox and legitimate by foreign Muslims, who had long viewed the movement with suspicion. Religion, faith, Islamic studies, Arabic, pilgrimages to Mecca, the *zakat* or tithe, hard work, and probity are stressed. Muslims are encouraged to get jobs rather than take welfare. Prison is still an important recruiting ground, for Wallace Muhammad, like his father and Malcolm X, had served in prison. Wallace's crime was resisting the draft as a conscientious objector in 1960. He served fourteen months in the federal prison at Sandstone, Minnesota.

Today there are an estimated twelve hundred blacks in prison who are Muslims. For every one thousand black prisoners in an institution, some two hundred are Muslims. About 80 percent convert while in jail. About three-quarters of American Muslims belong to the World Community of al-Islam, the others to sects such as the Ahmidiyya Muslims or the Sunni Muslims. Inter-Muslim battles have been set aside, and the groups work together. A number of prisons now have Muslim masjids, or mosques, with their *emans* (or imams) who are also prisoners; others are served by visiting *emans*. There is no stigma attached to being a prisoner among the Muslims, for Elijah Muhammad—and Malcolm X—had taught that all blacks were imprisoned in white America, whether they lived in Attica or New York City.

How many Muslims there are in the United States is unknown. Muslim figures, from different sources, are not clear. The FBI, which kept a close check on the Nation of Islam, used to put the figure at ten thousand or so instead of the hundreds of thousands claimed by Elijah Muhammad. Bilalian—black—Muslims say that there are about one million blacks—converts—who are Muslims, and half a million immigrants from Islamic nations, Muslim by birth.

Not all blacks who are Muslim belong to Wallace Muhammad's reformed World Community of al-Islam, however. In 1967, a member of the then Nation of Islam, Hamaas Abdul Khaalis, broke away saying that the movement was not orthodox. He had come under the influence of some Pakistani Muslims, and with

The various Muslim groups have made numerous converts among prison inmates, especially blacks. The new Muslims are extremely devout, praying (facing Mecca) five times a day, and following Islamic ritual to the letter. TONY O'BRIEN

their help he set up an American mosque of the Hanafis, one of the four "rites" or legal schools of orthodox Sunni Islam. Wallace Muhammad does not recognize the validity of the Hanafis. There has been some violence between the Hanafis and other Muslims, with resulting deaths. In 1958, Abdul Haleem Farrakhan, who had succeeded Malcolm X as the head of the Harlem mosque, Temple No. 7, denounced the "liberalized ideology" introduced by Wallace Muhammad. He announced the restoration of the "pure" faith of Wallace Fard and Elijah Muhammad, stating that blacks were being lulled into integration. If blacks didn't help themselves, said Farrakhan, they would find themselves "dead under the rabid heels of racism in the United States." Another group, the Allah Nation of Five Percenters, is also composed of former members of the Nation of Islam. They are led by God Kundalini Isa Allah, who believes that only 5 percent of the nation's blacks are capable of leading the black population. This self-styled elite group broke away from the Nation of Islam in 1957, but has not attracted much support. It is involved in several lawsuits over property in Harlem. In summary, Islam in America is centered around a solid core of blacks, devout and hard-working and socially conscious, who follow Wallace Muhammad and the now orthodox World Community of al-Islam.

9

☆　　☆　　☆　　☆　　☆　　☆　　☆　　☆　　☆

SECTS AND CULTS

WHAT OF THE OTHERS? THE SMALL CHURCHES, sects, and cults that claim the allegiance of a few dozen here, a hundred there, perhaps even a thousand scattered about, founded by charismatic saints, seers, masters, yogis, and gurus? The urge to have one's very own religion is a form of reaching for the ineffable. If two thousand years ago a village carpenter could be for many His Son miraculously conceived; if centuries later a monk could break with the Church of Rome to initiate the Reformation; if an upstate New York farm boy could be given a divine mission by an angel; or if a New England widow could heal miraculously; why not still another founder, and another, and another? Saints and seers proliferate upon the American scene, some authentic but failed, some charlatans, some even who do not know whether they are saint, fraud, or mere misfit. The wide span of this continent echoes with the sounds and images of past cults and sects, and reverberates today with new cults and sects beyond count.

To begin a study of sects and cults, the wonder woman named Jemima Wilkinson is an excellent example. She called herself the Public Universal Friend, a highly poetic title showing both great imagination and a vast appreciation of her role.

Jemima Wilkinson was born in 1752, the eighth of ten children of a pious Rhode Island Quaker couple. When she was about sixteen she became enamored of the New Light Baptists. Up to that time she had been a spoiled, frivolous child, who avoided school and avoided work on the family farm. When she was twenty-four she was expelled from the local Quaker meeting because of her New Light beliefs. Shortly after that she developed a fever, fell into a coma, from which she arose—she said from the dead—with the statement that her original soul had ascended into heaven and that her body was now inhabited by the "Spirit of Life," which came from God. Her duty was to warn a lost and guilty world to flee from His coming wrath. As a "Publisher of Truth," she had a Christ-like mission to preach repentance and the Second Coming. The doctor who had treated her stated that Jemima had in no sense died. He was bluntly contradicted by the new saint, and Jemima set about her mission of salvation.

She might have been imitating the Shakers' Mother Ann Lee, who was just beginning to proselytize in New England about this time. But Jemima had advantages Mother Ann lacked. She was an extremely attractive young woman; her looks clearly had a great part in her success. She was described as tall and graceful, with lustrous dark hair and penetrating black eyes. While Ann Lee was Mother or the Word, Jemima was the Public Universal Friend, and that may have seemed a title both warmer and less forbidding. The Friend soon had twenty followers. She set off to awaken Rhode Island and Connecticut to the coming millennium. The Friend wore men's clothing while astride a white horse, but she covered herself with a long flowing robe and rode slightly ahead of the faithful who trailed behind in pairs, keeping a respectful silence. Her goal, unlike that of Mother Ann, who sought out whoever would listen, was the wealthy and the educated.

In a few years the Friend had established three churches, well endowed by wealthy converts. The converts were probably attracted by her uniqueness rather than her preaching, which was an indistinct mixture of New Light doctrines, her childhood Quakerism, and her millennial expectations. Her greatest catch was the very rich Judge Potter, who built her a magnificent annex to his own mansion, turned over his entire estate, and let the Friend gain control of his household. Having stripped this fervent soul of most of his worldly possessions, the Friend unexpectedly announced that celibacy, hitherto ignored, was a leading doctrine. She called upon men and woman alike to join her church, to give up all, or rather, to turn all over to her. This path to salvation was not often welcomed by the public. Women in particular had no desire to see their husbands succumb to this charming otherworldly messenger. To stop criticism, the Friend announced that she was Jesus Christ in person, thus outdoing Mother Ann who was but the Second Coming in female form. New England became too hot for the Friend, and so she shifted her work to Philadelphia, where the Quakers, the dominant religious body, would have none of her.

The Friend eventually had to find new, virgin territory, and, in 1788, with the faithful and long-suffering Judge Potter, she moved to a large tract of land near Seneca Lake in upper New York State. Here she established the Shaker-like community of New Jerusalem. The land was fertile and productive. A school, sawmill, and gristmill were built, and, by 1800, Jerusalem numbered 250 souls. The Friend ceased her evangelistic work but was noted as a dynamic preacher, particularly at funerals. Dissension arose between the Friend and the Judge, who found himself trimmed of whatever material goods he still possessed. He left, holier than he had ever expected, but far poorer. The Friend, now well into middle-age, her beauty fading, began to show odd quirks of mind. Whatever she liked in the possession of someone else she demanded. "The Friend hath need of these things." And odd punishments were inflicted upon the erring. One sinner had to wear a black hood over his face for three months, another a bell on his coat. The Friend had reserved for herself a fine estate of 12,000 acres apart from Jerusalem. She lived in style there with a dozen select female disciples, and pondered the ungratefulness of her followers, who did not see that they would be rewarded in heaven for what they gave her on earth. Finally, ill, the beauty with which she had persuaded sinners to a path of salvation faded, the Friend died in 1819, aged sixty-seven. Jerusalem survived until 1863, the last disciple passing away in 1874.

Jemima Wilkinson was not alone in her odd path of saving sinners. Another mystic, by the name of Shadrach Ireland, had preceded her. For ten years he reigned over a sect which was a forerunner of the Shakers' communal life. In fact, he also preached doctrines which paralleled those of Mother Ann a half a generation later. Ireland was a millennialist, and he preached "perfectionism," having been influenced by the New Light minister George Whitefield, and celibacy. This doctrine, Ireland said, was for the present; when the millennium came, it would be abolished and male and female could practice their God-given instincts. However, while he enjoined celibacy in others, he took for himself a woman, Abigail Lougee, whom he described as merely a "spiritual bride." He had left his own wife and children behind years earlier in Cambridge. He built himself a retreat in Harvard (not to be confused with the site of the university). The building was raised in the night, so that it seemed to have appeared almost miraculously. It had a cupola from which Ireland could see the approach of strangers, and a secret staircase leading down to the cellar. Ireland had boasted to his followers that if he should die—a situation that his teachings indicated was unlikely—he would rise on the third day. Of course death came to him, and his followers waited expectantly in the cellar with the corpse. After a few weeks, resurrection still had not come. A period of disillusionment set in, followed by the conviction among the faithful that they had been deluded by a false messiah. The body was secretly buried at night in a cornfield to avoid the scorn and hostility of unbelievers.

During the period in which the Public Universal Friend and Shadrach Ireland flourished, a Canadian (whose name was never established) arrived in the States to proclaim that he was the True Christ. He allowed that he hadn't changed his clothes in seven years; still he attracted disciples, for, though he forbade marriage, he encouraged unlimited promiscuity, merely on the fact of his divine authority. But the messiah established some practices that separated male from female. Men had to eat standing, and women had to pray lying on their stomachs. The True Christ and his disciples wandered westward, looking for a site where they could lay out their version of the earthly Jerusalem undisturbed by puritan critics. The last word heard of them was in 1815 from the Missouri prairies, then inhabited by Indians who did not care for whites, whatever their theology and practices.

Such communities, whether sensible or not by other people's measurements, had vague utopian hopes of establishing the heavenly kingdom in the midst of a sinning world. A detailed accounting of the hundreds, if not thousands, of small groups thinking they had founded a heaven on earth would be redundant and boring. But some might be noted as examples of what attracted a few believers here and there.

Not all the communities were "Christian." The Brotherhood of the New Life, founded by Thomas Lake Harris in 1861, was soundly spiritualist in tone and belief. Harris, a former Universalist minister, took up Swedenborgianism in the 1850s. He announced in 1857 that he had been given the revelation not only of the spiritual but of the celestial meaning of the Scriptures. During this period, with the Reverend J. L. Scott, he had been living at Mountain Cover, Virginia, which he claimed was the very site of the Garden of Eden from which Adam and Eve had been expelled. No one had set foot there since the Fall. Scott told the faithful that he had seen words "printed in space" saying that he and his followers would be spared death. Harris and Scott soon parted, and Harris began again on the shores of Lake Erie. There were sixty disciples of the Brotherhood of the New Life which included a few daring Japanese and a large number of "ladies." One of Harris's prizes was a very wealthy gentleman named Laurence Oliphant, who came with his wife and mother. Harris conceived the idea of making wine to support the Brotherhood. It would not be "ordinary" wine, which teetotalers would object to, but a spiritual wine filled with the divine breath and therefore not intoxicating. Harris stated that God was both male and female, and like other prophets he preached celibacy for the faithful, but not for himself. He demanded complete obedience—"servitude" is the word often used by Harris—from his followers. And as in the case of Jemima Wilkinson's malleable judge, Harris soon relieved Oliphant of his wealth. Lawsuits followed, and Oliphant regained part of the money. Harris died in 1906. His followers, ignorant of their prophet's scorn for them, and his sexual practices, waited piously and patiently for his resurrection.

Not all communities were so exploitive of their believers. The Sanctified Sisters were a group of celibate women who were members of the Woman's Commonwealth, founded by Martha McWhirter in 1876. The group ran a boarding house, first in Texas and then in Washington, D.C., before they faded away after some two decades of pious work.

Other groups have faded away in the mists of history. Gone is the poetically named Spirit Fruit Society, a Christian commune founded by Jacob Beilhart in 1896. Little is known of it today. The biblically inspired Adonai-Shomo, founded in 1861 and surviving for thirty-five years, was centered around a now-nameless individual who claimed to be "Christ's Vice-regent." The Vice-regent's career ended when a grand jury indicated him for "revolting practices."

All too many founders, seers, and prophets had a touch of the profane about themselves. The once-famed House of David was virtually brought to its knees over a scandal involving Benjamin Parnell, who claimed to be the last of seven seers or messengers prophesied by Revelation 10. He was the first of the series to be an American (the others were English), and he established the House of David at Benton Harbor, Michigan, in 1903, as a "commonwealth, according to apostolic plan." The members were "Israelites," the lineal descendants of the twelve lost tribes of Israel. Parnell's Israelites turned over their worldly possessions to him, for he claimed to be the king of the community's spiritual and temporal affairs, and they even called him King Benjamin. To help support the House of David, Parnell established an amusement park at Benton Harbor, which for a period was a national attraction, much as Disneyland is today. Parnell also had a baseball team of some competence, which took on all comers in small towns in the Midwest and Northeast.

For biblical reasons, the male members of the House of David wear beards (something that helped make the baseball team famous), and never cut their hair. All are vegetarians. As Parnell explained the passage in Genesis, Adam was given "every herb bearing seeds" and every fruit of a tree, which "to you shall be meat." The men of the House of David never shave their faces nor cut their hair because Jesus did not, and they follow the ancient injunction that man is the head of woman, and the heads of women must "never be uncovered."

The House of David doctrines resemble those of other millennial sects, and they serve as a paradigm for a long list of minor churches that have risen and fallen with the ages. The members avoid the word "religion" because "there has been so much cruelty and bloodshed and all kinds of bitter strife under the name religion. We would rather say that we believe and teach the same doctrine of Jesus Christ . . . which Gospel was the redemption of the body." Sunday, said Benjamin, is "a type of the coming Millennial Sabbath Day. . . . A perfect creation of men and women are going to inhabit the earth during the Millennium and bring forth a perfect creation in the age of God." As with the Jehovah's Witnesses, "thousands of people now on earth will never die," for the House of David is convinced that they are living in the last 6,000 years of God's time, when the Lord will come to overthrow the wicked kingdoms of the earth. The signs are upon us, Benjamin pointed out in symbols used also by other millennial sects. Automobiles, telephones, radios, and motion pictures were prophesied in the Bible as signs of the end of the evil powers and of Satan's kingdom. The House of David, however, has an amusement park which has rodeos, dancing, billiards, midget auto rides, similar entertainment, and a vegetarian restaurant for tourists. They publish a monthly newspaper, *Shiloh's Messenger of Wisdom*, and keep in print various books assembled by King Benjamin, poetically titled but difficult reading for the unconvinced. Among them are *Rolling Ball of Fire* (three volumes), *Flaming Ball of Fire* (also three volumes), *The Book of Enoch*, and *The Book of Jasher*.

The establishment of the kingdom of God on earth never materialized. Charges of immorality and dishonesty were brought against King Benjamin. He died at the height of the scandal just before the Michigan supreme court exonerated him. Today the House of David is reported to have but 150 members left scattered about America, and an equal number in Australia, to carry on King Benjamin's message of the last times.

ORIC BOVAR AND FATHER YOD

Parnell, like most of the founders of sects and churches, claimed to be only a special messenger promised by Revelation. Yet there are those individuals who claim full divinity, to be Jesus Himself. What is astonishing is that they may often be believed.

One of the most recent self-proclaimed Christs was a man who called himself Oric Bovar, who headed a cult that reached a thousand members at its peak. Bovar had once been a rather prosaic American, born Richard Deane, about 1918, somewhere in the Midwest. He came to New York to be an actor, but aside from some minor roles in Hollywood and on Broadway, he could be considered a failure. About 1970, while living in Italy, he attracted some notice for his genius at drawing up astrological charts. He returned to New York, where people began to gather around him because of his keen insights into their personal problems and his ability to foretell futures. When he took a trip to Hollywood, his reputation had preceded him, and he gathered more followers. A sense of a divine mission took hold of Bovar. He put his followers on vegetarian diets; ordered them to abstain from sex, alcohol, and drugs; and warned of dire consequences for those who disobeyed. He arranged marriages between certain of his group but would not let the women seek medical help when pregnant.

After a few years he asserted that he was Jesus. Eventually

he said that Christmas would no longer be celebrated on December 25, but on his birthday, August 29. The cult was enormously successful financially, the members donating an estimated one hundred thousand to five hundred thousand dollars a year to their messiah. And they rather gullibly succumbed to his doctrines of undigested Hinduism (vague notions of karma and reincarnation) and a scramble of Judeo-Christian beliefs. But his demands on his followers and the increasing emphasis on his divine powers began to drive away the more perceptive. A newspaper reported one defector as saying, "He doesn't think he's Jesus anymore. He thinks he's God. He talks about my son, Oric Bovar." The membership dropped to about two hundred. Then a crisis struck. A young member, Stephanos Hatzitheodorou, a Greek-born immigrant, twenty-six years old, died of cancer in October 1976. Bovar ordered a vigil over the body, saying that Hatzitheodorou would rise from the dead. Day in and day out the disciples prayed over the body. Finally a woman who called herself Mary Magdalen phoned the police, not to inform on Bovar but in the expectation that their arrival would infuse the corpse with life again. The police found the dead man covered with a shroud, attended by six people chanting, "Rise, Stephan, rise."

Legally there was no crime; all the authorities could do was to issue Bovar and five followers a summons for failing to report a death to the police. At this point all but two dozen members abandoned Bovar. A court hearing was scheduled for Bovar and his people for late April 1977, but ten days before his appearance, Bovar leaped to his death from his apartment window. He left behind a handful of believers who are convinced that Bovar—Christ and God incarnate—will return. His death is their Star of Bethlehem, their Christmas, and their Easter. "Oric will come back," said one member to the press. "If they want him to, he'll reveal himself to them. He'll rise."

While Bovar was claiming to be Jesus and then God, a man on the other side of the continent, of almost the same age, was making an almost identical claim. In January 1975, a middle-aged man who called himself Yahowha (a form of Jehovah) brought a group of young disciples to Kauai, one of the Hawaiian islands. Yahowha called his cult The Source. The islanders were hostile to the members of The Source, so Yahowha migrated to San Francisco with his followers. He had recently run a health food restaurant in Los Angeles, The Source, after which his cult was named. But San Francisco did not seem ideal for The Source, so they moved again to Hawaii, this time to Hilo, where most of the one hundred members remained. With thirteen young women, three babies, and three men, Yahowha rented a massive beachfront home on the windward side of the island of Oahu.

Yahowha had originally been known as James Edward Baker. He had led a checkered life. He was supposed to have been a marine combat veteran of World War II, and he was an expert in jujitsu. After the war he tried several business ventures but all failed, except for a series of restaurants. Baker was known at first as a man who liked expensive things. He drove a Cadillac and wore white Italian silk suits. His first restaurant was the Aware Inn, then he bought the Old World, and, in 1969, established The Source. During these changes he became less of the typical West Coast entrepreneur and more and more of a mystic. He submitted himself at first to the disciple of a Sikh guru and then left, for he seemed to have believed himself beyond the teachings of his master. While he was engaged in this inner search, he divorced his wife, and was involved in incidents in which he killed two men with his bare hands during arguments. In the first case he was exonerated, in the second he was sentenced to three months in prison. Whatever mystical insights he gained brought him to a study of the Kabbalah, a Jewish, medieval, esoteric tradition. The Kabbalah is centered around the Divine Name of God—The Source of all. The Name is known as the tetragrammaton, Y H V H, the "Lost Word," for the pronunciation, according to Jewish tradition, was withdrawn by the Lord because of the sins of mankind. Baker now began to call himself "Yod, the Father" or active principle, for *yod* was the first of the four characters of the Divine Name. Young people, rootless and alienated from their families and from middle-class values, began to hang around The Source and listen to Father Yod. "We became a true family in spirit," said Astral, one of his later disciples. "We can't be separated. Jim Baker became

Father Yod, the ultimate father on earth." All fitted in with traditional Kabbalistic interpretations of the Divine Name, for with Yod as the Father, the next letter, H (*he*), was the mother, V (*vav*) was the son, and H (*he*) was the daughter. More and more young people flocked to The Source. As always, there was dissatisfaction. A defector, a member of The Source for a few months in 1972, called it "Hypocrisy." "It was communal living. Celibacy. But not really"—the same story found in other cults. Father Yod "was not evil; he was just on an ego trip."

Baker's ego led him from "Father Yod," the first letter of the Divine Name, to the Name Itself, to Yahowha, to "the ultimate Father." He was The Source in person, and his hold on his "children" grew. The members of The Source had complete faith in Baker as Yahowha. He gave them new names: Some of the women were called Isis, Ahom, and Lovely, and a man, Mercury. A woman, then in her twenties, Makusha, described herself as "Yahowha's mother." A male member of The Source told a newspaper reporter that the babies in the group were immaculately conceived offspring of Yahowha's.

At Oahu, the men of The Source took up hang-gliding, an exciting but dangerous sport. There seemed to have been a tenuous mystical connection between gliding and Yahowha's interpretation of Kabbalistic themes, for the "Divine Chariot" is a means by which the heart of the mystic ascends into the cosmos.

Mercury became an experienced pilot, gliding from 1,200-foot-high sheer cliffs near The Source's Oahu mansion into twenty-knot winds. He was so experienced and skillful that he was able to try for a world's hang-glider record. On August 1, 1975, at eight o'clock in the morning, Mercury strapped himself into his flimsy wire and rod frame and fabric wings, and stepped off the cliff into space, falling but suddenly rising as the trade winds caught the frail glider and lifted it into the skies. All day long, like some awkward primitive bird, Mercury rode the air currents above Oahu. On and on he glided, soaring, swooping, rising, and falling with the flowing air streams. The sun set, and he still was able to stay aloft. Then, in the gentle darkness, he quietly set down the glider on the beach about a mile from the mansion.

Reporters gathered around, to hear him say that he had never before had such an experience. "Incredible, to fly for that long, to see the sun come up, the sun go down, to fly in the dark, listening to the wind. It was the ultimate experience." Baker—Yahowha—had not been too impressed by Mercury's success. He had expressed the opinion that gliding would not be a popular sport, nor a popular mystical experience, for it took too much courage to step off the cliff. But still, there was that experience of the Divine Chariot, of ascending into the cosmos. Three weeks after Mercury's record flight, Yahowha, wearing his priestly robes, strapped himself into a glider and stepped off the cliff into space. For ten minutes the winds carried him, and then, unexpectedly, he plunged into the beach, the glider a mass of torn cloth and spars around his shattered body. But he was still alive. Gingerly, the faithful of The Source put him into a car and took him home. There were nine hours of agony. "It is not my will, Father, but Thine," Yahowha is reported to have said as he died.

For three and a half days the faithful kept the body of Yahowha in a vigil, believing it would take that period of time for the soul to leave properly. "God was released from that animal," said a disciple after the vigil.

The Source was to have still another tragedy. In mid-June the following year, Mercury took a night flight, stepping off the cliff into the sultry darkness. Shortly before eleven a crash was heard. Mercury was found at the bottom of the cliff, gasping in pain. He died as his fellow disciples attempted to bring him out. A witness informed the police, who demanded the body for an autopsy. The Source refused. Two nights later, fortified with the proper documents, an investigator for the city medical examiner's office and a squad of police broke down the door of the mansion and removed Mercury's body. Unfortunately, claimed the faithful, the soul had not had enough time to leave the body properly.

The small millennial sects seem to go out of their way to flirt with death, in the shadow of the approaching Last Days. In the states of Washington and Oregon, the Church of Armageddon, founded by a man who calls himself Love Israel, has tested the faith of its members in extreme terms. Love Israel, who says his church is based on the principles of the New Testament and is established as a "family," changed the names of his followers to Israel—Innocence Israel, Diligence Israel, and so on (including such names as Zeal, Enthusiasm, and Logic). Love Israel rules with a firm patriarchal hand. He has survived a number of unfortunate instances, one of which is the now familiar cliché of death and failed resurrection. During a ritual in 1972, two members of the Church of Armageddon, Solidarity Israel and Reverence Israel, inhaled fumes from tuolene, an industrial solvent, lost consciousness, and died. No aid had been given to the victims. Love Israel told his family that after three days Solidarity and Reverence would rise again from the dead. When they did not, he is said to have explained the incident away by stating that the two were "not strong of faith."

Deaths have occurred in other cults. The Glory Barn Faith Assembly, founded by Melvin Greider, a farmer, and Hobart Freeman, a theologian, in rural Indiana, drew a devout following of a thousand people who were attracted by Greider's preachings of the end of the world. Unfortunately, in the period between 1975 to 1978, two women members of the cult died in childbirth, and seven children passed away from other diseases because Greider and Freeman did not believe in medical treatment. Faith in the Lord was the cure. Freeman broke away from the Assembly, and Greider went on to plan underground houses where the Glory Barn members could survive the coming holocaust, in which, according to a report, "the credit card companies would put a laser mark on everyone's left hand."

NEW AGE WANDA AND THE UFO CULTS

Each age demands and creates its cult heroes and saints. Jemima Wilkinson was produced by the revivalism of the New Light movement. In this century, sect leaders like Wanda Moore, who called herself a "New Ager" and an "Aquarian Child," are the response to the space age. In 1967, after an apprenticeship in California with a motorcycle gang, Wanda retired to Greenwich Village where she established a hard-rock psychedelic club. Six months of ear-splitting noises and freaked-out patrons drove her into more meditative surroundings. In New Jersey she spent a year studying yoga and investigating spiritualism, reincarnation, and astral travel. She appeared again in public as New Age Wanda, with an aeon of mysticism behind her at only twenty-five, to became the guru and master of young (under thirty) entertainers and musicians.

New Age Wanda had a certain air of rationality about her. For considerable groups of people, the new age will be not on this earth but somewhere else in the universe. In 1975, a man and a woman known as Bo and Peep, or The Two, attracted a following who believed that Bo and Peep were two heavenly messengers whose coming was foretold in the Book of Revelation: "two witnesses" with the power to prophesy, whose message "tormented them that dwelt on the earth." These messengers in Revelation—apparently Bo and Peep (whose real names were Marshall Herff Appelwhite and Bonnie Lu Trousdale Nettles, both then in their mid-forties)—would be killed by angry disbelievers. Their bodies would lie in the street, and then they would rise from the dead after three and a half days. At this point Bo and Peep would lead their followers aboard a UFO and take them to heaven. Bo and Peep claimed to have come from outer space, but so long ago that they had forgotten what it was like. Their followers were estimated at three hundred to one thousand. Many gave up families, homes, and jobs to await the UFO. Bo and Peep told reporters that they had no desire to be killed; they wanted the "Demonstration," as they called their coming assassination, to happen as quickly as possible "so we could go back to our Father's kingdom and go on with our work there instead of here." The Demonstration still has not happened, and followers who gave up all they owned were faced with the problem of trying to reconstruct their lives again. In 1976, Bo and Peep videotaped their "final statement on earth," left it in Oklahoma, and disappeared with ninety-six select disciples. A sociologist who studied the cult says that three "families" remain behind, some sixty to seventy-five people awaiting the space ship to take them to the Father's kingdom.

Other UFO cults have surfaced. An Englishman named George King, born in 1919, into a family of occultists, claimed to have had visits from various divine figures, some five hundred in all, including Jesus and Krishna. He was especially guided by the "Space Brothers." As London was on the conservative side, King moved to the United States. He says that he is the psychic contact for one Master Aetherius, a Venusian, who speaks through him. Jesus and Saint Paul also speak through King. King easily attracted an American following. His center is now in Los Angeles. Such of his claims that he has ridden in a flying saucer with Jesus and the Virgin Mary are proof to his followers that he is in touch with the divine forces that will help defeat the evil powers in the universe that threaten the earth.

One more example of the many cults that center around beings from outer space will suffice. A woman whom researchers have given the name Mrs. Marian Keech reported that a mysterious being called Sananda sent her messages about the imminent destruction of part of the world by floods. Sananda was identified to Mrs. Keech as "the contemporary identity of the historical Jesus— His name having been adopted with the beginning of the 'new cycle' or age of light." Mrs. Keech—or Sananda—gained numbers of disciples, who, as in other cults, gave up worldly goods, careers, and families to prepare for the catastrophe and to be taken to "the Father's house" via flying saucers. After several false alarms about the imminent end, the cultists were at last able to establish that a certain Christmas was the true date. But, as always, the day passed without event, and the Sanandists are trying to recalculate their calendar.

The Swiss psychiatrist, C. G. Jung said (in *Memories, Dreams, Reflections*) that today, as at the time of Julius Caesar, whole people fear being robbed "of their cultural independence and of their autonomy, of being swallowed up in the mass."

Hence in many places there is a wave of hope in a reappearance of Christ, and a visionary rumor has even arisen which expresses expectations of redemption. The form it has taken, however, is comparable to nothing in the past, but is a typical child of the "age of technology." This is the worldwide distribution of the UFO phenomenon. . . .

THE PEOPLE'S TEMPLE

Whoever claims to be a messiah, a savior, or an incarnation of God descended to earth is usually self-appointed. Some "Christs" make the statement flatly and openly, others hint at it and let the faithful assume that the Divine is here and so they are to inform the public. Whether the leader is convinced of his divine role or is merely playing a part is often difficult to determine. Outsiders may assume fraud, or mental instability, but millions believe the True Messiah will return, as they are assured He will in Revelation and other scriptural texts. Meanwhile, as the Bible warns, false messiahs will delude the faithful.

Jim Jones, the leader of the People's Temple, stands out as a prime example of a "messiah" gone wrong. His followers said he claimed to be "Jesus Christ incarnate," and "the embodiment of God." He also claimed to be the Buddha and V. I. Lenin, the first dictator of Soviet Russia. Jones, born in 1931, grew up in a religious family in Indiana. He was ordained a Methodist minister when he was about nineteen, but was also affiliated for a time with the Unitarians. He soon founded his own unaffiliated church, the Christian Assembly of God, in Indianapolis. He lived simply and was noted for his work with the poor and minorities, and for his concern with social justice and peace. This involvement with social issues led him to change the name of his church to the People's Temple, which, under his active proselytization, attracted more and more members, mostly poor. His nursing homes for the underprivileged and the aged were said to be the best in Indianapolis. Because of his outstanding work, Jones was named the head of the Indianapolis human-rights organization.

In 1964, he quit Indianapolis, saying it was too racist. He had already begun to show signs of the mental instability and the egomania that became so pronounced later on. He had begun to demand sacrifices of his followers, asking not only for time and work but also for money. Some followers complained of Jones's sexual demands on women parishioners. On one occasion, in a tantrum, he threw the Bible on the floor and said, "People are paying more attention to this than to me." In 1964 or 1965, with some hundred followers, Jones settled near Ukiah, California. He soon had several thousand followers, about 80 percent of them black. About this time he began to assert that he was Jesus. After a brief period in Ukiah, he shifted the Temple to San Francisco. His messianic claims did not bring ridicule, but more and more converts instead. A touch of Marxism was added to his teachings, and he envisioned a Christian socialist state.

For years he had feared that "they" were out to get him. Who "they" were has never been clear; "Fascists," the FBI, and the CIA were mentioned. He also feared a nuclear war. So he decided to move again. He selected Guyana as the best place, for he believed that this remote, impoverished jungle land on the northeast shoulder of South America would be safe. Civilization there hugged a narrow strip of land along the sea coast, so Jones established his colony far inland. Nine hundred people—white, black, poor, middle class, old and young, with many children—followed him in blind faith in his messiahship to the new town of Jonesville.

But not all the members of the People's Temple were happy with the way Jones was leading them. There had been defectors in San Francisco, and in Guyana there was an undercurrent of unrest and uneasiness in people who objected to his harsh, even cruel rule, his obvious paranoia, his greed, and his sexual appetites. Not only did he inflict irrational and dangerous punishments upon people, but he demanded members' savings and property, and, men as well as women were prey to his sexual desires. Right before the end of the colony he boasted to his lawyer, Charles Garry, that he had just had intercourse with sixteen people—fourteen women and two men—in one day. A private army called the Angels kept people in order and punished "sinners." Jones's speeches, sometimes running to hours in length, were often incoherent. Open defections became common. In San Francisco, newspaper and magazine articles called attention to the strange cult. Finally, so great was the notoriety, that a committee headed by California Congressman Leo Ryan went to Jonestown to investigate the charges against Jones.

The result of that tragic visit stunned the world. After an ugly confrontation with Jones and some of his bodyguards, the visitors attempted to leave in their planes. But the Angels began to shoot. Ryan and three reporters were killed, and eight of the visitors were wounded. Garry and lawyer Mark Lane escaped unhurt. Then, after a long, haranguing speech, Jones, partly by persuasion, mainly by force, brought about the death of nine hundred members of the People's Temple by ordering them or talking them into drinking cyanide mixed in a soft drink. A few who were reluctant to die were shot by Angels, who later turned their guns on themselves. Jones had called himself the "Living God," but he, too, died with the others, in his case by a bullet wound. Whether he shot himself or someone else shot him is not known. The final count of the dead was 913.

The noted Baptist minister Billy Graham called Jones a "false messiah," as Jesus had warned (Mark 13:6), and said of the cult that "it would be a sad mistake to identify it in any way with Christianity." Graham ascribed its rise and fall to "Satanic forces." "It is all too easy to blunder into the arms of Satan," said Graham.

SATANISM

For some, Satanism rather than Christianity is the preferred way. Satanic cults have existed for centuries. Some are survivals of beliefs that predated Christianity; others are a deliberate attempt to turn away from the established churches onto other paths. Though some satanic cults are secret and closed to outsiders, the Church of Satan in San Francisco operates openly and welcomes notoriety. It has a tone of facetiousness about it, yet has a steady and loyal membership. The church was founded by Anton Szandor LaVey, a former musician, circus performer, and police photographer, who during these jobs developed a cynical view of human nature and of the hypocrisy of professed Christians. LaVey founded the church in 1966, on the following principles:

We hold Satan as a symbolic personal savior, who takes care of mundane, fleshly, carnal things. God exists as a universal force, a balancing factor in nature, too impersonal to care one whit whether we live or die. The sons, such as Jesus, take care of the spiritual aspect, but the Devil takes care of the carnal side of man.

We literally want to give the Devil his due. There never has been a
religion before that has given him credit.
   We don't have the turn-the-other-cheek concept. If some-
one does anything to us, we smash them.
   Satan represents indulgence instead of abstinence.
   Satan represents vengeance. . . .

Other Satanic principles are similar and oppose traditional virtues
and represent "all of the so-called sins, as they all lead to physical,
mental, or emotional gratification." Such an attitude attracts believers, but they must pay to join the church; initiation runs somewhere around five hundred dollars. LaVey doesn't want those who
have failed in other churches. He favors "accomplishment-oriented
people, who believe that the Satanic magic they perform will assist
them in gaining money, lovers, better positions."
   A more serious effort to build a church upon Satan was
the Process, founded in England by Roger De Grimston. The cult
had little success there, so De Grimston started afresh in America,
and gained a substantial following among professional people of
better-than-average education. He told potential disciples that the
traditional churches had failed, and, of great importance, that people were rarely able to communicate with each other. He spoke of
the problems of good and evil, and showed how opposites would
be reconciled. He developed a doctrine of the "Unity of Christ and
Satan," and brought together the "forces of Jehovah and Lucifer."
De Grimston's theology was complex, and many members complained that they could not understand it (it has borrowings, conscious or not, from the ancient Gnostic dualism of matter and
spirit, of light and dark). What everyone did comprehend, though,
was that the end of the world "as we know it" was coming.
   The first American Process center was founded in Boston,
and other churches soon followed in New Orleans, New York, and
in Western Europe. Members of the Process wore black capes and
gave out handbills in the streets explaining how they came to love
Satan. The church attracted a large number of young and rootless
people, many of whom had gone through the drug scene or had
tried yoga and Zen, occultism, Scientology, astrology, spiritualism,

and many of the other cults, sects, and fads that have been popular in the third quarter of this century. That the Process could have had a wider appeal seems unlikely in view of the strange and limited range of its tenets, which failed where other churches gave more rational explanations. For example, De Grimston said there are . . .

. . . the Three Great Gods of the Universe—Jehovah, Lucifer and Satan. . . . under innumerable disguises and descriptions, men have followed the three Great Gods of the Universe ever since the creation.

In this theogony Jehovah is "the wrathful God of vengeance and retribution," but Lucifer is "the Light Bearer," who "urges us to enjoy life to the full . . . to be gentle and kind and loving." Lucifer "has been mistakenly identified with Satan," for Satan is "the receiver of transcendent souls and corrupted bodies." Satan instills in man two directly opposite qualities, "at one end an urge to rise above all human and physical needs and appetites, to become all soul and no body," and at the other a desire to sink beneath all human values . . . to wallow in a morass of violence, lunacy and excessive physical indulgence." It is this lower aspect of Satan that men fear.

The Process preached a syllogism: Christ said to "love thine enemy," and since "Christ's Enemy was Satan and Satan's Enemy was Christ," we should love not only Christ but Satan.

The Process shared the common fear of the end of the world.

The Latter Days are upon us, and the prophecies for the End are now being fulfilled. . . . He who tries to live IN the world and be OF the world must die with the world. . . . This is man's last incarnation; his last chance to pay off all debts incurred both in this lifetime and all previous lifetimes.

Membership figures in the Process were secret, but small groups of the faithful, in their black capes, were seen in the major cities of the United States and Europe. A firm conviction that this was the right church was the shared belief of the members, for the Process was the "Church of the Final Judgment." However, a major and fatal schism hit the cult in 1974 when the greater number of the members rejected Satan, to begin again with the Foundation Church of the Millennium, with headquarters in New York. About 90 percent of the "ministers" and more than half the faithful left the Process. The strange mixed theology of Jehovah, Lucifer, Satan, and Jesus had become confusing. One of the schismatics, known as Father Lucius, one of the four "luminaries" or leaders of the Foundation, said, "We were confusing ourselves." The new sect "no longer tries to love Satan." But like its parent, it is millennial in belief and its members await the end of the world. The sect considers itself "almost Jewish," and uses a six-pointed star with a central design of two F's as an emblem. They observe the weekly celebration on Saturday. Unlike the Process, which celebrated in darkness lit only by candles, amid the fumes of incense before an altar with a stark Crucifix and the "Mendess goat" symbol of Satan, the Foundation observes its rituals in a coffee-house-like atmosphere, with violin, guitar, accordion, and drums.

HARE KRISHNAS AND MOONIES

That there is a religious upsurge in the United States has been noted not only by churchmen but by sociologists, the press and television, and the general public. This "religious renaissance" (as scholars call it) is nationwide. Polls and surveys can only suggest the immensity of the phenomenon. Projections and samples indicate that more than three million have recently joined the Pentecostal, born-again, and other charismatic churches. Perhaps at least six million Americans have been involved in the popular Hindu-inspired Transcendental Meditation movement (for which the individual pays a substantial sum for initiation, a mantra, and a few lessons in the techniques). The multitudinous schools of yoga have drawn some five million people, and "mysticism" (which covers a broad spectrum) has attracted an equal number. The various "oriental" religions—including the Theosophists, Bahais, the Hare

Krishnas, the Buddhist and Zen sects, and the American Sikhs, as prime examples—have gained about two million members.

Sects, cults, and churches tend often to congregate around otherwise mundane places like Ukiah, California, where for a while Jim Jones had his People's Temple. Now the town has attracted Moonies—the members of the Reverend Sun Myung Moon's Unification Church—as well as a Buddhist University (the City of Ten Thousand Buddhas), a Hare Krishna center, Mount Kalaisa, and, among many others, a group of devotees of Eckankar, the "Ancient Science of Soul Travel." The Hare Krishnas, once known as a peaceful sect founded in 1965 by A. C. Bhaktivedanta Swami Prabhupada, an Indian businessman, have for a long time been immersed in controversies over brain-washing converts and over their unusually heavy arsenals of weapons, among them grenade launchers and a machine gun at their centers at Ukiah and Moundsville, Virginia. Defectors have questioned the methods and practices used by the sect, but it continues to function in opulence and splendor, gaining the support of converts with substantial means. The Moonies, as a church founded abroad, have only a peripheral place in this account of American-born faiths. But they are noted for their aggressive proselytizing and the similarities in their beliefs, practices, and rituals that are common to many United States sects. The Moonies, who preach an apocalyptic doctrine of the Last Days, make intensive efforts to persuade possible converts through "love bombing" (unusual attention of a type the prospect may never have received from family, friends, and society) and "heavenly deception" (a weasel term, for lying in order to conceal the true nature of their goals).

The Soul Travelers, for the moment at least, seem to offer less danger to the unwary, except in matters of gullibility. Eckankar says it does not seek to take people from other religions ("We don't violate anyone's psychic space," says a member). It says it is "simply" a path to God for those who choose of their own free will to follow its teachings. Eckankar claims that its "teachings have existed for millions of years."

The present spiritual leader of Eckankar, Sri Darwin Gross, says he is the 972nd Living Eck Master in the world's longest unbroken line of teaching masters. His predecessors in the spiritual works of Eck include Pythagoras, who spoke of the "music of the spheres."

Eckankar draws heavily upon the more esoteric doctrines of Hinduism. One of its chief teachings is that of astral or soul travel. Cult members claim that one can travel "out of the universe" as easily as one can go from Ukiah to New York, for both the universe and New York are as much "here as there." Years of intense discipline are required to master soul travel—for "the mind must be stilled, because the mind is like a monkey on your back." The sect, like some others, likes to get its members young. Children from four to six can become Eck Teenies, the next group, to age ten, are Eck Tweenies, and so on. An adult membership costs seventy-five dollars and up, and a life membership one thousand dollars. In his adaptation of Hinduism, Gross "stands ready and waiting for those souls who are ready to travel back, to become again what we really are." This is similar to a doctrine preached by the Hare Krishnas, the illusion of the material world. "It is simply a dream, the God-world is beyond it." Reincarnation is basic to both cults. The Hare Krishnas say that "Those things we desire determine those things we become; if you are preoccupied with sex, you will return as a rabbit."

The sects and cults are as far-ranging as the mind and psyche can make them. Not only has the East been scoured for enlightenment, but so has Europe. Archaic and lost beliefs surface with regularity from out of the West's religious dust bin. The Wicca witches of the Mother Earth Church follow Baphomet, who, they explain, is an "androgynous witch deity who has horns, cloven heels and wings like Satan but who is beneficent instead." In Wicca, ritual sex is symbolic. An "*atheme*," or ritual dagger, is placed in a chalice of wine representing the sexual union that produces "Life." Ritual tools include jinx powder, Black Lucifer candles, Indian Spirit Uncrossing soap (to "dispel evil, attract good luck, or revamp energy"), Gypsy Witch fortune telling cards, and Tarot cards "to tap into the Universal Mind."

They go on and on, the cults and sects that attract and defy, help and mystify. That they have a widespread appeal to people mostly in the age group of eighteen to twenty-four is clear. The easy acceptance of even the most bizarre teachings, customs, and rituals has alarmed many people. Numerous efforts to "deprogram" cult and sect members have met with both approval and criticism. Defectors and apostates from some groups have had tragic stories to tell, and may work to help others still involved. Perhaps understandably, parents, who may have nothing to offer in exchange, want their children out of such cults as the Hare Krishnas and the Moonies and often enlist questionable aid. Also understandably, some cult members find nothing to attract them in the mainline churches, and they resent their parents' sudden interference in their new ways of life. Undoubtedly there are some cult members who in the long run are happy to be released from a temporary infatuation with a leader, master, guru, seer, or patriarch. But there is the question of basic liberties, religious and civil, which are sometimes infringed upon by the cults and sects to begin with, and later by parents and deprogrammers.

Undeniably the current religious renaissance is hardly a sometime phenomenon. What is happening today runs squarely in the American tradition, which witnessed the Great Awakening of the early eighteenth century; the revivals of New England and the Appalachian frontiers; the birth of such churches as the Shakers, Mormons, and Christian Scientists; the various millennial sects; Pentecostalism; the American Indian and the black Islamic movements; and the growth of Methodism and the expansion of the Baptists, both totally different churches from their English and European counterparts.

Whatever the church or sect, whether Christian, millennial, Indian, or Islamic, there is an expectation of a golden age, when the grass is green, the forests are lush, water runs cool and clear, and mankind is well fed and happy. The sinners will have received their old-fashioned American come-uppance, and the elect will bask in the glory of the Messiah in the earthly Jerusalem. In their literature, the various churches, though unrelated and often hostile to each other, show a remarkable similarity of image in their visual representations of the new world: Father, mother, brother, and sister stroll through a peaceful meadow, while the sun, symbol of the Almighty, sparkles through the branches of the nearby forest that fringes the pastureland.

The millennialism of past ages has found a welcome in many sects. To many millions of people it is evident that the signs of the times—wars, social unrest, famine, and drought, newly erupting volcanoes—represent the end of the ages and the arrival of the Messiah. For many it seems that man has nowhere to lay his head except in the charismatic arms of a self-proclaimed God, Jehovah if not Jesus, or of a divine messenger, come to bring hope and redemption to believers.

RELIGIOUS ORGANIZATIONS

It would be impossible in the space available to list all the denominations in their many variations that this book has discussed (the Baptists groups alone number over thirty). Many important bodies outside of this work are also omitted, among them the Roman Catholics, Eastern Orthodox, Presbyterians, Quakers, Jews, and so on. The best single source for information and addresses is Frank S. Mead's *Handbook of Denominations in the United States* (Abingdon, Nashville).

Here are addresses of some church groups mentioned in the text.

Advent Christian Church, P.O. Box 23152, Charlotte, North Carolina 28212

Assemblies of God, General Council, 1345 Boonville Avenue, Springfield, Missouri 65802

Church of Christ, Scientist, 107 Falmouth Street, Boston, Massachusetts 03100

Church of Jesus Christ of Latter-day Saints, 47 East South Temple Street, Salt Lake City, Utah 84111

Church of Jesus Christ (Temple Lot), Temple Lot, Independence, Missouri 64000

Divine Science Church, 1400 Williams Street, Denver, Colorado 80218

General Church of the New Jerusalem (Swedenborgian), Bryn Athyn, Pennsylvania 19009

House of David, P.O. Box 1067, Benton Harbor, Michigan 49022

International Church of the Foursquare Gospel, 1100 Glendale Boulevard, Los Angeles, California 90026

Jehovah's Witnesses, 124 Columbia Heights, Brooklyn, New York 11201

Muslim Islamic Center, 2551 Massachusetts Avenue, N.W., Washington, D.C. 20008

Reorganized Church of Jesus Christ of Latter-Day Saints, The Auditorium, Independence, Missouri 64051

Seventh-day Adventists, 6840 Eastern Avenue, N.W., Washington, D.C. 20012

United Church of Christ (a body including the major groups of Congregational churches), 297 Park Avenue South, New York, New York 10010

Unity School of Christianity, Unity Village, Missouri 64063

FURTHER READING

These are the best of a wide assortment of works about all the various faiths, and are the most easily obtainable. For further information, the inquirer might write directly to the denomination's headquarters. Normally, material is free, and ample.

AHLSTROM, SYDNEY E. *A Religious History of the American People.* New Haven: Yale University Press, 1972. A very basic and wide-ranging work.

ANDREWS, EDWARD DEMING. *The People Called Shakers.* New York: Dover, 1963. One of the most comprehensive and sympathetic studies of the Society.

BEAL, MERRILL D. *I Will Fight No More: Chief Joseph and the Nez Percé War.* Seattle: University of Washington Press, 1963.

BROWN, DEE. *Bury My Heart at Wounded Knee: An Indian History of the American West.* New York: Bantam, 1972. A classic account.

CARDEN, KAREN W. AND PELTON, ROBERT W. *Snake Handlers: Good Fearers or Fanatics?* New York: Nelson, 1974.

————. *They Shall Cast Out Devils.* New York: A. S. Barnes, 1976. Both titles are full but uncritical.

CLARK, E. T. *The Small Sects in America.* Nashville and New York: Abingdon-Cokesbury Press, 1949. A basic work.

DELAFIELD, D. A. *Ellen G. White and the Seventh-day Adventist Church.* Mountain View, CA: Pacific Press Publishing Assn., 1963. By a member of the church.

DELORIA, VINE, JR. *Custer Died for Your Sins: An Indian Manifesto.* New York: Macmillan, 1969. The Indian side of the great massacre.

EDDY, MARY BAKER. *Science and Health, with Key to the Scriptures.* Boston: The First Church of Christ, Scientist, 1903. Christian Science in the founder's own words; necessary reading for an understanding of the doctrines.

FREEMAN, JAMES DILLET. *The Story of Unity.* Rev. ed. Unity Village, MO: Unity Books, 1979. By a member of the Unity staff, and uncritical.

FURNAS, J. S. *A Social History of the United States 1587–1914.* New York: G. P. Putnam's Sons, 1969. Excellent background material of the times in which many of the American-born faiths were founded.

HILL, CHRISTOPHER. *The World Turned Upside Down.* New York: Penguin, 1972. Levellers, Ranters, early Quakers, and others seen from the viewpoint of the participants in the great English religious revolt.

HOLLOWAY, MARK. *Heavens on Earth: Utopian Communities in America 1680–1880.* New York: Dover, 1966. The search for the Earthly Jerusalem, in a multitude of forms, by saints, seers, and crooks.

HUDSON, WINTHROP S. *Religion in America.* Rev. ed. New York: Scribner's, 1973. A historical account of the development of religious life in this country.

Jehovah's Witnesses in the Divine Purpose. Brooklyn: Watchtower Bible and Tract Society of New York, 1959. A history of the Witnesses and their doctrines by staff members, not to be read unquestioningly.

KEARNEY, CLARENCE J. *The Advent Christian Story.* Published by the author, 1968. One of the major groups to come out of the Great Disappointment.

LABARRE, WESTON. *The Peyote Cult.* Rev. ed. New York: Schocken Books, 1968. A detailed and sympathetic study; important.

————. *They Shall Take Up Serpents: Psychology of the Southern Snake-Handling Cult.* New York: Schocken Books, 1974. Again, a masterly study by a sympathetic scholar.

LANTERNARI, VITTORIO. *The Religions of the Oppressed: A Study of Modern Messianic Cults.* New York: Knopf, 1963. Prophetic movements in the United States and elsewhere by an Italian sociologist. Unfortunately, the work is marred by avoidable errors and, though important, is not always to be relied upon.

MEAD, FRANK S. *Handbook of Denominations.* 6th ed. Nashville: Abingdon, 1975. A comprehensive guide to major and minor churches and sects throughout the United States, their history, doctrines, organization, and present status.

MERTON, THOMAS. *Mystics and Zen Masters.* New York: Farrar, Straus and Giroux, 1967. Contains an essay about the Shaker colony at Pleasant Hill, Kentucky.

MOONEY, JAMES. *The Ghost Dance and the Sioux Outbreak of 1890.* Washington, D.C.: U.S. Bureau of American Ethnology. Annual Report XIV (1892–93), Part II, 1896. *The* great work about the Ghost Dance and the tragedy of Wounded Knee. The report has been reprinted by various small presses from time to time, and can be found with some searching. Mooney includes similar movements in other cultures, notably England, where the Jumpers and Ranters were so prominent.

MORGAN, LEWIS H. *League of the Ho-de-No Sau-Nee or Iroquois.* New York: Dodd, 1901. A famous work by an early anthropologist who lived among the Indians of New York State; background of the Good Message.

NORDHOFF, CHARLES. *The Communistic Societies of the United States.* 1875. Reprint. New York: Schocken Books, 1965. One of the first studies of religious and secular utopian groups.

O'DEA, THOMAS F. *The Mormons.* Chicago: University of Chicago Press, 1957. By a non-Mormon.

ROSTEN, LEO, ed. *Religions of America.* Rev. ed. New York: Simon and Schuster, 1975. A guide and almanac of major denominations, with apologias by members of the churches listed.

SCHOLEM, GERSHOM G. *On the Kabbalah and Its Symbolism.* New York: Schocken Books, 1965. The Jewish mystical movement.

SMITH, JOSEPH, JR., trans. *Book of Mormon.* Salt Lake City: The Church of Jesus Christ of Latter-day Saints, 1952. "An account written by the Hand of Mormon upon Plates taken from the Plates of Nephi."

SMITH, JOSEPH FIELDING. *Essentials in Church History.* Salt Lake City: Deseret, 1972. The "church" is the Mormon, and no other; Detailed, but one-sided.

SWEDENBORG, EMMANUEL. *A Compendium of the Theological Writings of Emmanuel Swedenborg.* New York: Swedenborg Foundation, 1977. Johnny Appleseed's source.

TOMLINSON, IRVING C. *Twelve Years with Mary Baker Eddy.* Boston: The Christian Science Publishing Society, 1945. By one of her closest associates.

VOGEL, VIRGIL J. *This Country Was Ours.* New York: Harper & Row, 1972. A documentary history of the American Indian in excerpts from official and nonofficial papers.

WILBUR, SIBYL. *The Life of Mary Baker Eddy*. Boston: The Christian Science Publishing Company, 1907. An "official" biography.

WILSON, EDMUND. *Apologies to the Iroquois*. New York: Farrar, Straus and Giroux, 1960. Excellent material about the Good Message and its celebration today.

INDEX